020

# THE

# Subversive Manifesto

Text copyright © Jonathan Bartley 2003
The author asserts the moral right
to be identified as the author of this work

**Published by**
**The Bible Reading Fellowship**
First Floor, Elsfield Hall
15–17 Elsfield Way, Oxford OX2 8FG

ISBN 1 84101 211 4
First published 2003
10 9 8 7 6 5 4 3 2 1 0
All rights reserved

**Acknowledgments**
Unless otherwise stated, scripture quotations are taken from the Holy
Bible, New International Version, copyright © 1973, 1978, 1984 by
International Bible Society, are used by permission of Hodder & Stoughton
Limited. All rights reserved. 'NIV' is a registered trademark of International
Bible Society. UK trademark number 1448790.

A catalogue record for this book is available from the British Library

Printed and bound in Great Britain by
Bookmarque, Croydon

# Subversive Manifesto

*Lifting the lid on God's political agenda*

Jonathan Bartley

*For Samuel*
*Though not yet through your first year of life,*
*you have already given me enough love to last a lifetime*

## ACKNOWLEDGMENTS

So many people have been so helpful in so many ways during the writing of this book that it is not possible to name them all.

Special thanks, however, must go to Noel Moules, the Anvil Trust and the Workshop course, which has been the inspiration for so much of this book. Lloyd Pietersen, Linda Gill and Chris Smith were also invaluable in their gentle correction and advice.

Most of all, I want to say thank you to my wife, Lucy, my mother and my father, who have all been so patient with me. It is only their love that has kept me going.

# CONTENTS

# FOREWORD

The church faces a moment of opportunity—a *kairos* moment.

*Kairos* is a Greek word used in the New Testament to mean 'now is the time' or 'God's appointed moment. It could also be used in the law courts when a lawyer wisely selected exactly the right moment to press his case; and in archery it meant pressing through an opening to strike a target. A '*kairos* moment' is a time of opportunity when God issues the Church with a challenge to decisive action.

Jonathan Bartley has identified that the Church in our generation is facing just such a moment.

Following the tragic events of 11 September 2001, it was amazing to see how, in the desire to find meaning in a desperate situation, it was the Church that was turned to by many people. This is perhaps what might be expected—but the Church's contribution did not end there.

As discussion continued about what the most appropriate response would be, and a 'war on terrorism' was launched, the churches again were often at the centre of the debate—this time offering words of warning as much as words of comfort.

When the time came to consider an attack on Iraq, issues about whether such a conflict could be considered 'just' were uppermost in people's minds. Bishops led the way with their reservations about the morality of a war. Church leaders from the UK came as a delegation to meet with the British Prime Minister to plead for restraint. Tony Blair went to the Vatican to try to persuade the Pope that a war with Iraq would be just. The Pope, unconvinced, sent his envoy to try to persuade George Bush not to take military action.

Neither is it just in the field of international politics that the contribution of the Church is being recognized. Whether it be church schools or the provision of welfare within local communities, governments are seeing the vital work that the churches do on the ground and taking account of that when they make their policy. Faith works, and the policy makers are beginning to understand this fact.

Within the Church, too, there is growing awareness that the Church has a political mission—and that this isn't just an 'optional extra'. Throughout the Church there is a movement—a subversive movement—going on, which is awakening people to the political dimension of their faith. It may soon seem absurd that we ever thought the gospel didn't have a direct application to politics. Our practice of stripping the Bible of its political message is, after all, at odds with many other cultures and many other times in church history.

But the Church now faces an important decision. We stand at a crossroads, and must decide which road to take. This book lays down a challenge to the Church—not just to those who belong to political parties, but to everyone. But we should be under no illusions. *Kairos* moments can be missed. We can fail to heed the call.

This is a time when the Church needs wisdom, courage and a sense of urgency. It needs wisdom to discern possibilities and to make adjustments. It needs courage to accept God's calling for changes and urgency about its reason for being. It is not a matter of new windows, different colours or new logos and slogans. It is not a new façade to feed our pride. It is about who we are—about substance, not rhetoric.

To describe themselves, the New Testament Church chose another Greek word—*ekklesia*. It was perhaps surprising, because this was not a religious term. It was, in fact, a secular, political term used to describe a gathering of people called for a political purpose.

The early Church recognized that their mission was political as much as it was spiritual. The challenge to us is whether we are prepared to make the same bold and subversive statement that they made.

Steve Chalke
Founder, *Oasis Trust* and *Faithworks*

# Chapter 1

# Biblical Emasculation

Shortly after I left university, I went to work as a researcher in the House of Commons. One night I found myself opposite a Member of Parliament over dinner. She had a sincere faith and before long the conversation drifted towards spiritual matters. We began discussing the parable of the good Samaritan, but as the meal went on, it slowly dawned on me that hers was no traditional interpretation. My jaw nearly hit the table when I finally realized the point that she was making. For her, the parable of the good Samaritan was a story that underlined the importance of a capitalist economy.

You could be forgiven for wondering how such an interpretation could be gleaned. I certainly wondered. The explanation went something like this. The Samaritan needed to have personal wealth in order to help the poor unfortunate left beaten and robbed by the side of the road. If the Samaritan had not been free to exercise his spirit of free enterprise, he would have had no cash, and so no help to offer. The parable therefore illustrates well the virtues of the market economy and how, by generating wealth, everyone can benefit.

It seemed strange to me, and still does, that Christians who have chosen a career in politics can pick up the Bible and completely miss the political dimension that is staring them in the face. It is even stranger when they try to read into the text a political meaning that just isn't there, but that has consistently been my experience of working for a number of years in and around Westminster. Although the Bible is a book about kings, laws, judges and wars, although the central message of Jesus' ministry is of a new kingdom, and the biblical language is dominated by talk of power and authority, it is almost as if any political content has been stripped out from the canon of scripture and discarded as entirely irrelevant.

Although my political view is somewhat different, I have a sincere respect for the particular Member of Parliament whose story I have just told, and, indeed, the many other Christians who work in and around the House of Commons. They have an extremely difficult job to do, and most do it to the best of their ability. Like so many of us, however—and I include myself in this—when it comes to matters biblical they display a tendency common to those both inside and outside the corridors of power. We might call that tendency 'biblical emasculation'.

A few years before I began my work in Parliament, I joined a missionary organization. As is the habit with 18-year-old males, I developed a bit of a liking for one of the girls on my team. Her name was Bethany. Nothing romantic happened between Bethany and me (indeed, there were strict rules about that kind of thing) but that didn't stop me wondering. On more than one occasion I found myself flicking through the pages of the Bible, speculating about whether God would tell me that I was going to marry her one day. Looking back on it, it seems absurd, but it was very real at the time. It was a particular problem, given the number of times 'Bethany' is mentioned as a place that Jesus frequented. It was all I could do to stop myself trying to find some double meaning—some twist implying that God was revealing to me that she would be my future wife.

Whether we are politicians or police officers, bus drivers or businessmen or women, we all like to go to the Bible for a bit of therapy. In fact, if we're honest, that's often the main reason we pick it up and browse through its pages. Perhaps we need guidance on a major life decision. Maybe we are feeling down and want some encouragement. It might be that we want moral direction on how we are living at the moment. The reasons are numerous but the approach is usually the same. It's all about us, our own lives, our own needs—ourselves.

The Bible can be a great and very real source of comfort and guidance, but for many of us, that is the only way that we come to the Bible. Even when the reason is not introspection or self-examination, when we read a passage of scripture our first reaction is to relate what we read instantly to our own personal lives, and apply what we find in a very individualistic way.

In doing this, however, we are stripping the biblical text of its power. By focusing on only one dimension—the personal—the gospel message is being emasculated.

# A privatized ideology

Part of the reason for such widespread biblical emasculation is the set of values, the perspective, with which we approach the text. The MP's interpretation of the parable of the good Samaritan, of course, misses the point of the parable entirely. She did not let the Bible speak for itself, but instead used it to support her own personal perspective. The story is not about free market economics or the importance of riches—far from it. But because of where she was coming from—because of her own ideology—she had read a new meaning into the text.

It is easy to be critical of what seems like an abuse of a biblical story, but we are all guilty. We all come to the scriptures with our own biases, our own emphases and our own agendas—even if we like to think that we don't. Let's stop for a minute to consider what most 'normal' people sitting in their churches on a Sunday morning might make of the parable.

When we hear a sermon on the subject of the 'good Samaritan', we are invariably told that it is a story about helping those around us. It is a story about fulfilling our responsibilities and loving our neighbours. We might be exhorted to give more to charity, or perhaps to get to know the people in our street better. We might even see it as a challenge to rethink the way we treat our colleagues at work. By the time the sermon has finished and we head home for

Sunday lunch, we are firmly resolved never to walk by on the other side again.

Can you see what has happened? Our first thought has been to interpret the parable in personal terms. We have read it in the light of what it means for our *own* behaviour and private lives—but what about a more public application?

To begin with, why do we apply the lesson about helping others only at an individual level? Isn't this parable in fact a story about nations helping nations, and continents helping continents, as much as about one-on-one charity? The story is, after all, a direct challenge to the nationalism of Jesus' day that put the interests of Israel before those of other nations.

What does this parable mean for us today concerning our response to the countries lying beaten and bleeding by the side of the information superhighway or the traffic in arms sales? There are implications for issues such as immigration and asylum too. This is a story about a Jew being helped by someone from another land who would have been treated as an inferior. Does this tell us anything about the way we should be treating immigrants and asylum seekers, or persecuted minorities beyond our shores?

Then there is the significance of the people who are singled out in the parable by Jesus as those who walked by on the other side. Why did Jesus name them? If he had to use public figures, why wasn't one a rich tax collector? Is the reason perhaps that the priest and the Levite were important political figures and it was their duty more than anyone else's to care for the vulnerable? Jesus seems to be publicly identifying powerful figures as failing in their responsibilities for those in their care. He names and shames the powerful for their failure to look after the vulnerable. The challenge to the powers would certainly not have been lost on the hearers in the highly politically charged environment of Jesus' day. But will it be lost on us?

The parable of the good Samaritan is not, then, just a gentle encouragement to care for our neighbours and make sure we don't 'walk by on the other side'. It is a devastating critique of the powerful, and a story that should leave us working through a host of public and political implications. No wonder the stories that Jesus told sent the world around him into turmoil! The parable of the good Samaritan, like so many in the Bible, is a story with teeth.

Rarely, though, do we hear that kind of interpretation in church on a Sunday morning. It is far safer and less controversial to stick with the lesson in personal morality. It is safer for us, and for the world around us, but it also robs the parable of its power.

Interpreting and approaching the Bible in purely personal terms is a bit like buying a television set but only ever watching a small selection of programmes. You might watch some cookery programmes and brush up on your culinary skills. If you're feeling down, you might watch a sitcom. In need of a bit of ethical guidance? You could turn on a morning chat show for the day's moral dilemma. But the TV is not there just to make us feel better about ourselves. If we let it, it will begin to tell us a story (albeit often sanitized and biased). It will inform us about what is happening beyond the safety of our front doors, where we are going, and how people are relating to one another—not just in our own local communities but at an international level. The news bulletins, documentaries and current affairs programmes all open up a whole new dimension and perspective on the world.

That new dimension can be uncomfortable, because once we know what is going on, there are implications and consequences. If we watch the coverage of a general election campaign, we have to think about who we are going to vote for. If we see pictures of a famine in Ethiopia, questions are immediately raised in our minds about what we can do to help. When we see a nuclear weapon tested, we realize that we have the capability to destroy ourselves.

It is the same with the Bible. We can stick with our personal and private readings of scripture that keep us on the straight and narrow, or we can begin to realize the power contained within the amazing accounts, stories and ideas that make up the biblical canon—and once we grasp that the stories are so much more than personal, a whole new world opens up for our faith.

# Political renaissance

Is a political reading of scripture just an optional extra, though—
something that we can undertake to enrich our faith and deepen
our spirituality if we want that sort of thing? Some might say that
the Bible is so full of treasure, it is unlikely that we shall ever get
anywhere near understanding just a fraction of it, so perhaps we
should be content with our private approach. After all, if it isn't
broken, why fix it? Provided we are happy and content in our
relationship with God, why look to make things more complicated?

I want to suggest that the situation in which we find ourselves
with a purely private reading of a scripture is a little more serious
than that, particularly when we consider what is going on around us.

While the way that the majority of Christians read the Bible is
still very much in personal terms, at the time of writing this book
something quite remarkable is happening in the UK. We are seeing
nothing short of a renaissance in terms of Christian, and particularly
evangelical, involvement in politics.

For the first time in many years, all three main party leaders
profess a Christian faith, to the point where they have been making a point of addressing major evangelical events such as Spring
Harvest. Each of the main parties now has a strong Christian
grouping within it. The Conservative Christian Fellowship is even
based at its party's Central Office, having been brought into the
hub of things through the 'Listening to Britain' initiative started by
William Hague. The Fellowship was even asked to set up a special
unit there, and its director was put in charge of pulling together the
Conservative manifesto at the 2001 general election.

Within the Labour party, since Tony Blair became Prime Minister
it has become almost fashionable to be a Christian Socialist. The
Christian Socialist Movement (CSM), although over 150 years old
(even older than the Labour party) has also undergone its own
renaissance. The former chairman and co-ordinator both became
MPs in 2001. At one time, as much as one quarter of the Labour

Cabinet were members of CSM, and Christian Socialism is now an established and respected strand of thinking within the Labour Party.

The Liberal Democrats, although a relatively new party, also have their own Christian grouping—the Liberal Democrat Christian Forum—firmly established. A number of their prominent MPs speak openly about their faith, and there is now a Christian campaign grouping within the party.

Nor has the renaissance been limited to the corridors of power and the party machines. Outside Parliament there has been an apparent explosion of activity, with dozens of organizations attempting to make their mark. Christian movements, lobby groups, campaign groups and think-tanks are all now in existence, covering almost every issue imaginable, from Third World debt to the arms trade, from child poverty to abortion and the family. Britain even saw its first 'Christian' political party contest the elections for the London Assembly in 2000.

Compared with the situation just 20 years ago, when there was little if any talk of Christian engagement, there has been a staggering reawakening of Christian interest and involvement in politics. This book will not explore the reasons for the renaissance, but it is this re-engagement with politics that makes the failure to recognize the political dimension of the biblical story so serious. While the reawakening is perhaps to be welcomed, at the same time it could carry terrible consequences if the political dimension of the Bible continues to be ignored.

History is littered with tragic examples of the way that Christians have abused power and engaged in political action with dreadful results. Apartheid, the Spanish Inquisition, the oppression of women, the slave trade—there is no end to the ways in which the Bible has been misused and misappropriated politically with disastrous consequences. We should not be so arrogant as to suppose that we can't repeat the disasters of the past. If we are not careful, we will again use the scriptures as nothing more than legitimization for our own political positions rather than seeking to allow the Bible to shape our political views. With the best intentions in the world, the Christian faith can all too easily be used to back a cause, which can lead to results that are very far from the intentions and purposes of God.

## Rethinking revival

There is a more important reason why we must come to terms with the political dimension of the scriptures—one that has implications for all of us, not just for those involved in public life.

Soon after the 1997 general election, I went away for a weekend in the country with a small group of young Christian leaders. The event was hosted by two people who wanted to encourage Christians in public life, and who had themselves held important political positions. At the beginning of the weekend they sat us all down and said that they had a very important message to deliver to us. 'We've been praying about what we should say to you,' they said, 'and we feel that the most important thing we can impart to you can be summed up in one word.'

We were all on the edge of our seats. Here were two men whom God had placed in high public office, influencing the nation for good—and God had given them a message for us. What was this great word? What was this mysterious secret that God had revealed to them? 'That word,' they continued, 'is "revival".'

Since that time I have been to meeting after meeting, event after event, conference after conference where 'revival' has been the solution put forward to the nation's, if not the world's, problems. For thousands of Christians, whether they be in public office or not, 'revival' is indeed the answer. But is this really the final word about how God wants to move in the country's national life?

The Bible tells a story of kings, judges, laws, justice, economics and policy-making. It tells us that God's purposes for both private and national life go way beyond spiritual renewal. God cares about spiritual reawakening, but not for its own sake. God cares about it because it is a part of the divine plan, but only a part. Until we recognize the fullness of the vision that the Bible gives us, our efforts will fall far short of the richness into which God wants us to enter. Indeed, taken in isolation, we will misunderstand what it means to be spiritually reawakened.

I realize that I am on dangerous ground here. Revival is now an industry in and of itself. Christian bookshops are stuffed full of books on the subject. There is an endless flow of videos, tapes and magazine articles about it. Thousands, if not millions, of Christians have placed their time, energy and hope in it. 'Revival' for many people is what the Christian faith in 21st-century Britain is all about.

I want to suggest, though, that this is not the entirety of God's agenda. God does have a vision for how things will be changed, and a programme for how it will be achieved, but that vision has less to do with 'revival' than we would like to think—at least, not in the way that many people hope and pray for.

The vision that God has is more exciting, more powerful, and more complete. It is a vision that doesn't just change people's hearts, but changes the way that societies are run, economies are structured and legal systems are organized. It is a political agenda in the fullest sense of the word.

## Rediscovering God's politics

It is perhaps worth saying at this point that when I use the word 'political' I do not mean the stuff of party politics, or indeed anything much to do with what goes on at Westminster. I use the word in three senses.

Firstly, God's agenda is political in its broadest sense—I mean the stuff of life, the world beyond our front doors. 'Politics' in its truest sense is about how society is organized. It is about how economies are run, health care is provided and criminal behaviour addressed. It is about relations between nations and neighbours. It is about how we deal with terrorists and how we treat our children.

In short, politics is about how we order the world that God has entrusted to us.

Secondly, God's agenda is political because it is about who has power and authority. Satan, we are told, has authority in this world (2 Corinthians 4:4). Yet at the same time we know that it is God's universe. Here is a political intrigue that goes to the very heart of God's unfolding plans. But these are not abstract spiritual concepts; they are ideas that have a very real bearing on how we make sense of the world, and how we behave in it.

Lastly, God's agenda is political in the sense that much of the salvation story is based around political scenarios. It has been pointed out that perhaps the major part of Exodus, Leviticus, Numbers, Deuteronomy, Judges, Kings, Chronicles, Nehemiah, Esther, Isaiah, Jeremiah, Ezekiel, Daniel, and many of the 'minor' prophets have a dominant political story. Genesis, Psalms, Proverbs and Ecclesiastes, and most of the other books in the Hebrew scriptures, have substantial political content. In the New Testament, Jesus' engagement with the powers is central, and the dominant theme of his teaching is a new kingdom. The crucifixion is a politically engineered event. Half the chapters of Acts cover political confrontation in Jerusalem, most of the epistles contain political teaching and Revelation is steeped in political imagery.[1]

Sadly, the political agenda in all three senses is all too often missed, but a narrow and private view of the gospel like the one that I have already highlighted leads to very narrow and private answers to the world around us. It is time to rediscover the fullness of the gospel message, the political gospel—that the gospel is good news to all of creation, to our hospitals and our prisons, to our town halls and businesses, our rural and urban environments.

This book, therefore, is not intended for a small minority of Christians involved in national politics. Its message is something that every Christian must embrace, understand and act upon. God's political agenda is relevant to you if you are a carer or an engineer, a roadsweeper or a brain surgeon, a lawyer or a homemaker. It is relevant because it goes to the very heart of what it means to be a follower of Jesus Christ. To be a follower of Jesus is to be political—whether we like it or not.

# A depoliticized faith

In the West, the political content of the Bible—a book with 3,000 references to kings or kingdoms—has often been missed completely by many people, but this is not the case the world over. It has been said that the notion that biblical Christianity has nothing to do with politics is, in fact, 'little more than a Western Christian aberration'.[2] At most other times and in most other cultures, the fact that the biblical story is political would have been taken for granted.

In countries like South Africa or South America, where political oppression has been all too apparent, the Bible is frequently seen as a profoundly political book with wide-ranging and formidable consequences. Archbishop Desmond Tutu has famously said, 'Which Bible do people read when they say, "Don't mix religion and politics"?'[3] It is hardly surprising that those who find themselves on the receiving end of such 'dangerous' politics as Tutu espouses are quicker to find out what the Bible says on the matter than those of us who feel relatively unaffected by political decision-making.

Perhaps one of the primary reasons for the depoliticization of the biblical story in the West is that we still view politics as something 'out there'. As Britons, we live in a country where politics is still the domain of only a few, with its own language and its own culture. For most of us, the word 'politics' conjures up images of middle-aged men yelling at each other across the floor of the House of Commons, rather than anything related to our everyday lives, with a bearing on who we are.

But of course politicians do have an amazing effect on the way we live our lives. They determine how fast we can drive, how much we take home in our pay packets, how our children should be educated, and what standard of health care we will receive.

They set the standards for socially acceptable behaviour, and decide what happens to those who deviate from the norm. They decide when we should fight, and whom we should kill or let live in times of war.

The strange thing is that most of the time we just leave the politicians to get on with it. Despite the amazing power and control that they wield, our contribution is usually confined to turning out every few years to cast a vote. We may occasionally demand lower taxes and better services, but that is about it. Our society has been depoliticized. We have abdicated responsibility and control over our lives.

The situation is little different when it comes to our faith. A firm wedge has been driven between religion and politics. The original reasons why this is the case can be traced back to the intellectual movement of the Enlightenment. Previously, religion and politics had gone hand in hand—often with disastrous consequences. The English civil war had at its heart both politics and religion, and in many people's minds it was religious zeal that was responsible for killing the king. The result was a determination by Enlightenment philosophers such as Thomas Hobbes (1588–1679) and John Locke (1632–1704) to create a basis for politics and the ordering of society that did not rely on God. Religion was taken out of the equation and a new basis for political authority established that did not depend on a personal God.

None of this, though, was what God intended. We are political beings, made in the image of a political God. We were never supposed to abdicate responsibility for our lives to others in this way. We were never meant to accept our faith as relating only to private, inward matters. When we accept this agenda, our faith is emasculated and God's vision for the world is stripped of its power. When it comes to matters of public life we have nothing to say. Our mission becomes saving as many people as we can from eternal damnation and from a dying world, rather than recognizing our role in stewarding the creation and witnessing to the re-establishment of God's authority over the whole earth.

# Returning to our roots

At the times when the various parts of the biblical canon were written, however, any distinction between religious and political life would have been quite alien. As we have noted above concerning the parable of the good Samaritan, the religious leaders of Jesus' day also exercised political power. The Law of Moses was (in part, at least) the law of the land as well as the powerhouse for the Jerusalem economy. The Sanhedrin was the major arm of domestic government and the Jerusalem authorities were ultimately responsible to the Roman governor.[4] This was far from an apolitical situation. Politics and religion were in many cases inseparable, and faith was firmly in the public domain. Once we recognize this fact, a whole new perspective on the Bible opens up. Let's look at another story that Jesus told, to illustrate the point.

In Luke's Gospel is an account of the parable of the ten minas. A man of noble birth goes away to become king, but before he goes he calls his ten servants to him and gives them some silver coins. 'Put this money to work,' he says, 'until I come back.'

Soon the man returns home having been made king, and sends for the servants to find out what they have done with the money while he has been away. The servants who have made money are rewarded. But the servant who, out of fear, did nothing with his mina is condemned. In fact, he has his money taken away and given to the one who made the most. The king concludes by saying that those who have lots of money will receive more and those who don't obey him will be killed (Luke 19:11–27).

Is this another parable about wealth creation and the free market? We all know the interpretation well. The hero is the king, whom we usually think of as Jesus. Another hero is perhaps the servant who made a lot from what he was given. The villain, on the other hand, is the man who did nothing with his money, who is seen as idle and undeserving and who reaps the consequences of his actions along with all the other rebels.

Most people have interpreted the parable as being about wise stewardship and using your talents wisely. We are like the king's servants, and must be good stewards of what we are given. We are to make it grow and multiply 'for the kingdom'. We are to be obedient to the king, and we will be rewarded.

But take a moment to think again. Is that really what the parable is about? First, we must recognize the context. This is a highly politicized situation. The story is placed right before Jesus' triumphal entry into Jerusalem. The people are waiting for a Davidic king to come riding in to deliver them from Roman oppression and tyranny and establish God's kingdom. Jesus is going to be greeted as Israel's liberator. In fact, the Gospel writer himself confirms that this is why Jesus is telling the story: 'He went on to tell them a parable, because he was near Jerusalem and the people thought that the kingdom of God was going to appear at once' (Luke 19:11).

Second, we know what Jesus' concerns were. Jesus knew that his kingdom was not going to be one of violent revolution, but of service and sacrifice. He knew the warnings that God had given to Israel about choosing a king hundreds of years earlier and how the king would oppress the people (1 Samuel 8:11–18).

Now think about the king's actions in the parable. They are fundamentally unjust. The king finishes by saying, 'To everyone who has, more will be given, but as for those who have nothing, even what they have will be taken away.' This is a huge contrast to the message that Jesus has been preaching and demonstrating for the last few years of his ministry. It is not a message of grace. The story ends with the king asking for all his enemies to be brought before him and killed. Is this really how Jesus would have portrayed himself?

Could it be that this is *not* a parable supporting a Protestant work ethic? Is it, in fact, the servant who challenges the king's authority who is the hero? To be in line with the biblical view that kings are often oppressive and exploitative, the king could not have represented Jesus. Instead, the king would have been the villain of the tale. Rather than a parable about stewardship, it then becomes what Luke suggested it was—a story about God's kingdom. It is a warning against power and its abuse, as the people continue under the false expectation that Jesus will take the throne by force.

Suddenly, what we have always interpreted as a parable about multiplying what we have to make more becomes what Luke said it was all along—a parable about the kingdom of God. In the context of a political reading of scripture, the story takes on a completely different meaning, and a meaning that may well make more sense.[5]

Of course, for those of us who really don't care about politics, or have never suffered at the hands of an oppressive regime, it is not surprising that we do not see the political dimension. If, however, we were peasant farmers labouring under a dictatorship, we might hold a very different perspective.

## Uncovering God's agenda

So where does this leave us today? How do we begin to understand what God's political agenda really is? It is, of course, to the Bible that we must turn, but we need to turn its pages with care.

We all have a tendency to consider passages of scripture in isolation, apart from the rest of the Bible. But as the parable of the ten minas shows, we need to consider each passage in the context of the whole salvation story. To understand God's kingdom, we need to come to terms with how God views kings, for example. To make sense of Jesus' stories, we need to grasp his mission and purpose.

The Bible is not a set of instructions that we can flick through like a car manual, to find the chapter to sort out our latest problem. However, it is instructive.[6] The salvation story gives us an understanding of God's character—God's values, aims, objectives and purposes. God didn't just create the world, stand back and watch it turn. God speaks and acts within it.

The Bible is also the story of God's people. There is a unified strand that cuts through the artificial barriers of Hebrew history,

New Testament and church history, revealing how God's plan is being outworked through a community. As we come to terms with God's agenda we also find our own place within that community. Where do we fit in, and what is our role and function—our mission in God's unfolding drama?

For many years there has been debate about whether our mission as Christians is political or not. Some have seen it as nothing but political, trying to change society by more 'Christian laws'. Others have stripped our mission of all political meaning, advocating complete withdrawal and focusing on saving souls. Others still have tried to walk a 'third way' that marries the two perspectives—trying to make 'Christian' laws while converting people 'apart' from politics on the ground.

I want to suggest that all of these approaches are inadequate. We are not called to a 'third' or even a 'fourth' way. What we are called to follow is the 'whole way'—a path that draws no artificial division between evangelism and social action, or preaching the gospel and political involvement. The Bible doesn't draw those distinctions, so why should we?

It will become clear, I hope, during the course of this book, that God's political agenda is quite unlike the political agenda of the political parties and the agenda of many political Christians. This is not a book about power so much as powerlessness, not about domination so much as service, not about imposition so much as submission.

I will also suggest that God's agenda is not only political but entirely subversive—subversive to the way the world works around us, but also to our local churches. It will turn our world upside down, delivering a message that will bring down the powerful and shake the way that the world works. Such is the subversive nature of God's manifesto.

To begin to understand God's political agenda, however, it is to the biblical story itself that we must turn.

## NOTES

1   I am indebted to Dr Alan Storkey for his brief survey of the political themes in the Bible in an unpublished paper, 'The Bible's Politics'

2   Richard Bauckham, *The Bible in Politics: How to Read the Bible Politically* (SPCK, 1989), p. 1

3   'Now that we are free—a conversation with Desmond Tutu', interview by Norman Boucher, *Brown Alumni* magazine, Vol. 99 No. 4, March/April 1999

4   C. Marshall, *Kingdom Come: The Kingdom of God in the Teaching of Jesus* (Impetus Publications, 1990)

5   The interpretation comes from a base community in Solentiname, Nicaragua. See Ernesto Cardenal, ed., *The Gospel in Solentiname*, 4 vols. (Orbis, 1982), 4:38–48. For a slightly different reading, using the concept of nobleman with retainers rather than Archelaus, see William R. Herzog II, *Parables as Subversive Speech: Jesus as Pedagogue of the Oppressed* (Westminster/John Knox, 1994), pp. 150–68

6   Bauckham, p. 6

# Chapter 2

# The Subversive Manifesto

At the start of every general election campaign, amid the flashing of photographers' bulbs, myriads of microphones and the jockeying of journalists, the political parties compete to be the first to launch their manifestos. These documents set out not simply their proposed programmes for running the country but the very *way* that the parties will govern, should they be elected.

The launch of God's manifesto would put even the most elaborate public relations exercise to shame. In a blaze of glory God announced his purposes for the world that had been created:

*Let us make human beings in our image, in our likeness, and let them rule over the fish of the sea and the birds of the air, over the livestock, over all the earth, and over all the creatures that move along the ground... Be fruitful and increase in number; fill the earth and subdue it. Rule over the fish of the sea and the birds of the air and over every living creature that moves on the ground (Genesis 1:26, 28).*

From the very beginning it was God's intention that human beings would share and enjoy all that had been made. They were to increase in number, spread out and fill the earth, and cover every part of it. They were not to be passive recipients. With this glorious gift was to come a special authority. Setting out a radical model of devolution and empowerment, God made it clear that he was not going to hold on to the power alone. In addition to enjoying all that had been made, human beings were to be God's agents. They were to be God's government. Made in the image of God, humankind was to exercise the same loving management that God had demonstrated in the creative act of making the world and everything in it.

Such an amazing vision stands in stark contrast to the understanding of power and authority popularly held today. We are used to political parties competing to take as much power as they can so that their programmes can be driven through. God, however, empowered and trusted people with all that had been made. Instead of keeping a tight grip on the reigns of power, God allowed those created human beings to have stewardship and control over everything that had been so lovingly crafted.

## The Opposition attacks

It is perhaps easy in retrospect to criticize God's decision to give human beings authority over creation, but it would, no doubt, have gone perfectly if it hadn't been for the presence of one factor—the Opposition.

Most manifesto launches are bound to meet with a political backlash. The other parties who want to take the power for themselves set political traps, pointing to inconsistencies in policies, and highlighting 'black holes' in programmes. God's manifesto was to suffer the same fate. The Opposition was quick off the mark, and determined to undermine the divine plan with a scheme designed to make the implementation of the manifesto impossible.

The Opposition approached God's new appointments and suggested that information was being withheld (Genesis 3:1). God, it was alleged, was not giving Adam and Eve everything that they should be getting. Did they really have total authority over the creation if there were still things that they were not permitted to do?

Having sown the seeds of doubt, the Opposition made them an offer that they couldn't refuse: 'If you just eat of the tree, then you will really be like God' (Genesis 3:5). The created could become equal to the creator.

In an act of rebellion and an abuse of the power and responsibility that they had been given, Adam and Eve fell into the trap. The effects of this move by Adam and Eve were to become all too apparent as God launched an inquiry into what had gone wrong. The damage was serious. In place of the harmony of the created order came conflict. Adam tried to 'name and shame' Eve. Eve avoided personal responsibility and public apology by blaming her environment (Genesis 3:11–13). Nor did the consequences end there. With God's government in disarray, the problems spread and turned to violence as Cain murdered his brother Abel (Genesis 4:8).

The manifesto appeared to be lying in tatters. It would have been difficult for even the most optimistic observer of the time to see how God's agenda could be carried out now that the very people who were supposed to govern were at each other's throats.

Finally, so pained by what humankind was doing, God appeared to pull the plug on the whole plan. The waters that God had separated and held back in creation were let go in a flood, and most of humankind was wiped from the face of the earth.

## The campaign revives

For most people, this would probably go down as the most disastrous manifesto launch in history. A shrewd eye might have spotted, however, that God's campaign was not 'dead in the water'. In a very subtle way God's political agenda was still moving forward. God hadn't abandoned his plans for humankind and the creation. Indeed, human beings were still very much at the centre of his purposes for the world.

When Adam and Eve left the garden of Eden, God provided physical protection in the form of clothing (Genesis 3:21). When Cain killed his brother Abel, God limited the escalation in violence that might have resulted from a blood feud, by protecting Cain with a mark (Genesis 4:15). Even when God wiped human beings from the face of the earth, he saved Noah and his family (Genesis 7—8).

Perhaps the best indication that God's plans might be on track came from an unlikely source. Against this backdrop of social unrest, family breakdown and violence, God's first politician emerged.

Ask the average Christian to name the first king in the Bible, and the chances are they might mention Saul, or even the king of Sodom (Genesis 14:17), but he is, in fact, a man by the name of Nimrod, who we are told was 'the first on earth to be a mighty man' (Genesis 10:8).

Following the Fall, the primary concern of human beings had ceased to be stewardship, and had become instead survival against an extremely hostile environment. As the relationships between human beings and the creation worsened, violence rather than harmony became the hallmark of life in those far-off times.

It has been suggested, however, that Nimrod stood out from his contemporaries as someone who was able to protect the people from the new external threats (Genesis 10:8–12). In so doing he demonstrated an authority reminiscent of that given by God to Adam and Eve, but also the loving care that God continued to show to humankind.[1] In contrast to the violence and domination that had resulted from the Fall, God's manifesto intentions for the world were still very much alive.

## The manifesto unfolds

In order to demonstrate that their manifesto proposals will work, politicians often point to examples or models of best practice on which their ideas are based. When formulating new policies, a government will similarly look to pilot projects to 'test the water' and give an indication of the direction that the policies should take.

At this point in the salvation story, however, examples of best practice for how God's manifesto was going to be brought to fruition are still few and far between. Most people were still following patterns of violent conquest rather than colonization. Groups of people, such as those at Babel, maintained that it was better to centralize power, staying in one place and making a name for themselves rather than spreading out across the earth (Genesis 11:1–9).

But one man who was continually on the move was the nomadic tribesman Abraham, and it was to him that God's attention now turned. Abraham was to be the father of a nation of people who would have their own land and enjoy God's blessing. They would be God's people, and through them God would begin to make things right again. But this would not be for their own sake. This people would be used to bring blessings to the whole world. The children of Abraham would be kings and form new nations (Genesis 12:2; 17:6). The suggestion seemed to be that through Abraham's descendants God's authority would somehow be re-established.

For all intents and purposes, Abraham's immediate descendants got off to a fairly good start. Political intercourse continually took place with their contemporaries and they stood out as people of peace and justice, avoiding clashes with neighbours where possible. Abraham even pleaded on behalf of the nations around him, attempting to avert the destruction of Sodom and Gomorrah for their economic oppression, surplus affluence, violence and failure to help the poor and needy (Ezekiel 16:49). But although growing in wealth and numbers, they still seemed a long way from being a nation and fulfilling the promises that had been made. In fact, it wasn't until the time of Abraham's great-grandson, Joseph, that nationhood looked like a real possibility.

## God's chancellor

No one could deny that Joseph's political career was a rocky one. From his boyhood he had dreams of power, and they caused him significant problems, particularly where the rest of his family was concerned.

Joseph's dreams seemed to imply that his brothers were somehow inferior to him. Along with the favouritism that his father Jacob showed, this was too much for his siblings. Perhaps they remembered the promise made to their ancestor Abraham that from their family would come kings. They may have worried that Joseph would become too powerful. Whatever the reason, his brothers decided to get rid of him. Selling him into slavery, they staged an elaborate cover-up (Genesis 37:5–35).

Joseph ended up in the foreign land of Egypt, serving one of Pharaoh's senior officials. Showing aptitude, he soon started to make a name for himself, and became what we might consider today to be the official's private secretary. A promising career, however, seemed to come to a premature end. Falsely accused of a sexual scandal, he was sacked, discredited and put in prison (Genesis 39:4, 7–18).

The outlook once again looked bleak. If this was God's path to creating a great nation, it certainly seemed a strange way of going about it. Even in jail, however, Joseph's skills began to show through. Impressing the prison authorities, before long he was virtually running the place.

While in prison, Joseph came across two civil servants who had previously worked for Pharaoh. Both were troubled by dreams, something of which Joseph had considerable experience. Under God's guidance, Joseph interpreted the dreams, and predicted that one of the men would be put to death while the other would be reinstated to his post.

Sure enough, Joseph's interpretation came to pass, and as a result he once again found himself in high office. The civil servant who regained his position remembered Joseph, and summoned him in as a special adviser (Genesis 40:1–23).

As he had done in almost every circumstance before, Joseph thrived in his new position. Under God's guidance, his economic forecasts turned out to be remarkably accurate. He predicted a boom in the economy followed by a major economic downturn and crisis. On the basis of his predictions he was put in charge of the economic affairs. He subsequently formulated a policy to take Egypt through the difficult times ahead, including creation of a new governmental position and boosting the country's reserves by twenty per cent during its boom years (Genesis 41:34).

For perhaps the first time, there was clear evidence that the plan revealed to Abraham was coming to pass. It was not so much the ups and downs of Joseph's political career that were important. Rather, it was the fact that Joseph saved the known world from a terrible famine by shrewd economic planning. In this he was following the original creation mandate of stewardship. He acted as protector against the ruthless consequences of the fallen creation, but he also fulfilled in part the mandate given to Abraham. Not only was he blessed, but he was a blessing to the nations around him. Once again God's authority and government of the world through humankind were looking like a credible policy.

# Yahweh delivers

By this point in God's unfolding campaign, things seemed quite promising. Hopes were raised even further when Joseph's family arrived in Egypt as economic migrants. They were given the best land, and top jobs. As time moved on, their descendants became numerous as had been predicted, and they filled the whole land of Egypt (Genesis 47:5–6; Exodus 1:6).

Another threat to God's manifesto was soon to come, however, from the very highest levels. Feeling that his own power was in question, and afraid that the children of Israel might turn on the nation, the new Pharaoh enslaved the Hebrews and their cries for justice were ignored. Nor did the ruler of the Egyptians stop there. For political expediency, and playing on political fears dressed up in the national interest, a policy of state-sponsored genocide was introduced. A birth-control programme was put in place to destroy male Hebrew babies (Exodus 1:9–11, 15–16).

There was ample evidence, though, that God was going to look after his people. First, the implementation of the policy was thwarted by employees in Egypt's health care sector. The midwives simply refused to carry out the ruthless population policy (Exodus 1:17). God also had a plan for the liberation of the Hebrews, in the form of Moses, a Hebrew child who had grown up in Pharaoh's household.

Although he was not one of the greatest political orators, the battle that ensued between Moses and Pharaoh was one of the greatest political skirmishes of the Bible. The struggle was between the God of justice and Pharaoh's system of slavery and domination. It was only after bargaining, numerous policy U-turns and a series of concessions that the Egyptian government, and with it its system of control and oppression, finally caved in and let the people go free.

But that is not the whole story. By the time the political bargaining was over, the nation that Joseph had helped to prosper was left socially and economically battered. Not only were the Egyptian farming industries devastated, but the Hebrews left the country, taking large quantities of the Egyptian gold and currency reserves (Exodus 9:6; 10:13–15; 12:35–36).

By any standards, what took place in Egypt was a remarkable political event. By the end there was no doubt that the God of Abraham still had authority over the mightiest of political rulers and most violent of regimes; but it was still not clear how the pledges made to Abraham were going to come true. How exactly was God going to bring about the promises to make the Hebrews into a nation?

## The policy detail is announced

There comes a time in every election campaign when a manifesto has to be costed. Policy details are listed, and precise measures are outlined for how a political programme is to be realized. Sinai was to be the place where much of this was to take place for Abraham's descendants. In the equivalent of a modern-day press conference, God began to reveal exactly what kind of nation Israel was to be.

As a basis for the plans, attention was drawn to God's track record (Exodus 20:1). Yahweh had already acted out of mercy and justice, and the law was to be an extension of these qualities. The Hebrew law was for the people's own welfare and something that they should choose to take on, not something that was being imposed upon an unwilling population. Indeed, the detail was explained with an elaboration of the promise made to Abraham. If Israel followed through on what God was suggesting, things could only get better.

Laws were set out that looked after the poor, the vulnerable and foreigners. They involved debt cancellation, a ban on interest, and family rights. The children of Israel were also to remember God's act of liberation and mercy in their dealings with the nations and foreigners around them. God had shown them justice and they were to do the same in their dealings with others beyond their borders.

By the time the Hebrews arrived in the land promised to Abraham, the politics of oppression and exploitation from the gods of Egypt had been dismantled. Yahweh had been revealed as the God of freedom, justice and compassion.

Although there had been a huge new development in terms of God's plans, a great deal seemed to hang on the fact that Israel apparently couldn't stick to the laws that had been set out at Sinai. Indeed, there is little evidence that many of the laws that God gave to Israel were ever carried out. Not surprisingly, during the time in the wilderness and the centuries that followed in the promised land, Israel was beset by problems, not least in its foreign policy. Even after the Israelites had conquered their homeland, the people were still plagued by attacks from the surrounding nations.

Nevertheless, during all this time Israel still managed to display some of the uniqueness that God required—particularly in its constitutional settlement. Unlike the hostile nations around it, Israel had no king except God. Any other political leadership and authority was diffused among the elders. When the nation was in peril, under attack or under threat, God continued to help them by raising up agents to do justice, in the form of 'judges'.

For a while, the political arrangements seem to work, but by the time of the last great judge, Samuel, the policy of constitutional uniqueness was showing considerable signs of strain. The pressure of living without a human king proved too much to bear. In the face of external military threat, Israel demanded change. In a desire to impersonate the systems of the countries around them, the Israelites took on a king (1 Samuel 8:6).

Such a demand was clearly against the policy prescription of God's manifesto. Indeed, God interpreted this decision as a rejection of his authority (1 Samuel 8:7; 12:17). However, such was the nature of God's agenda (as demonstrated so clearly in Eden) that God allowed Israel the choice.

The only stipulation was that Israel should be warned of the consequences of its choice. Samuel was obedient, and pointed to the state control, including slavery, taxation and military conscription, that would inevitably result (1 Samuel 8:11–18). Nevertheless, Israel did not heed the warning and went ahead with its plans. The tribal confederacy gave way to a centralized monarchy.

## The corruption sets in

So where did this leave God's unfolding plans? There is no doubt that, once again, the credibility of God's manifesto was being called into question. God's nation was intended to be a beacon to the world of how God's government should operate, but it seemed to be losing its distinctiveness.

The temptation for the new kings of Israel to abuse their position of power was indeed too strong. The undoing of the first king, Saul, was his jealousy and paranoia. He became obsessed with defending his power and capturing his heir apparent (1 Samuel 18:9). His successor, David, despite being a brilliant politician, laying strong foundations and putting the nation on the map (2 Samuel 11: 1–20), used his position for sexual conquest and even murder. In three generations, by the end of the reign of David's son Solomon,

God's warnings about the consequences of choosing a king had come to pass.

During the time of the first three kings, there was a glimmer of hope, however. God made a covenant with David that one of his 'house' would rule for ever (2 Samuel 7:16). Such a promise kept the hope of Israel alive, not just during the times of constitutional change, but in the centuries that followed.

By the end of Solomon's reign, the promise seemed an enigma. What has been termed a 'golden age' in Israel's history brought wealth only to a few, and slavery, taxation and drudgery to the majority. The country ran up enormous debts as expenditure exceeded income, and the huge building projects became a liability. Instead of one of David's descendants taking the throne and establishing God's rule, the empire fell apart and was replaced by two rival states—Israel and Judah.

## God's campaigners

It is unusual, to say the least, for a political party to point out where its own manifesto is falling short. It is hard to imagine any party chairman turning the spotlight on its own failings and highlighting where its commitments are not being realized. But this is exactly the kind of thing that God seemed to be doing.

This development came in the form of the prophets. The prophets were a remarkable feature in the unfolding of God's manifesto, not least because the main agents that God had seemed to be using were political leaders and politicians. But while political authority did indeed rest with the kings, true authority more often rested with what we might call today 'social commentators'.

The Hebrew word for prophet means literally 'one who communicates'. Nowadays the word conjures up images of someone who may foretell the future, but this was secondary in the mission of the biblical prophets. First and foremost they were God's spokespeople. It is perhaps useful to think of them as a cross between journalists and lobbyists, their business being public affairs. It was their job to point out, often publicly, where the nation was falling short of the standards that God's manifesto required.

Most prophets faced real hostility from the kings of Israel, and often the people too. They needed to be good communicators, and their style gave maximum impact in the minimum amount of time. Indeed, hostility often led the prophets to use acted prophecies or poetry so that their messages would gain public attention.

Prophets had, of course, been in existence since the first great prophet—Moses. But by the time the kingdom was breaking down, a new era of prophecy was dawning. This in turn brought a new political style. Campaigners with no prophetic background would arise and speak to the nation in time of crisis. They would take issue with the politicians, and then disappear into the background. In a kind of media terrorism, they would get in, deliver their message, and get out with maximum impact, often leaving chaos in their wake.

After the sudden appearance of Elijah before King Ahab (1 Kings 17:1), prophecy would never be the same again. The stark difference between Elijah and the slick 'professional' prophets of his day was his identification with the poorest peasants, through his appearance. Other prophets, such as Amos, laid before Israel a devastating economic critique. The rich lived in extravagance, but only a few enjoyed the wealth of the nation while the poor were ground down with injustice—and the legal system favoured those with money. Micah brought an agricultural perspective, drawing attention to greedy landowners and cruel judges who all supported social injustice for personal gain. Time after time, the campaigners highlighted the shortfalls in the life of the nation.

But the message was not all doom and gloom. At the same time as the inadequacies in the life of Israel were being pointed out, a new hope began to emerge. The suggestion that seemed to recur again and again was that God still had one more measure in the manifesto to announce.

The prophet Micah spoke of days of love, when God's rule of peace would be universal. Isaiah similarly saw present events as part of the great divine purpose of history, and not only the history of Israel but that of the other nations. Again Jerusalem would become God's city, with righteous judges and a king after God's own heart, making covenant life a reality.

The expectation began to form that God would intervene as had happened in Egypt, and two important events would take place. The cosmos would be rid of evil once and for all, and God's reign of peace would again descend. In short, all things would once again return to an Eden-like state, and the world would be made right once and for all.

## The election broadcast

The manifesto was still to face even bigger tests, however. A crisis ensued as Assyria invaded the north and Israel's political history came to an end. Many fled to the southern kingdom of Judah, but most were scattered or taken hostage. Israel returned once again to the oppression it had experienced in Egypt. Eventually, Judah would follow, and even the great city of David, Jerusalem, would be reduced to rubble.

Where had God's promise gone? Israel was supposed to have been a blessing to the world, but now the nation had disappeared. How were the prophets and the people of God to have faith and confidence in Yahweh's control of time and history when everything was going so wrong?

The answer lay, at least in part, in the events of the exile. Despite their oppression by foreign nations, some Israelites found favour with the ruling governments and managed to influence their situations in the way that Joseph had done in Egypt.

One such person was Daniel. Along with a few high-born Jewish children, he was taken as a hostage to Babylon. Daniel himself did not have the standing of a prophet. He was a statesman, a politician, and accordingly found himself along with his friends as a special advisor to the Babylonian government.

Through Daniel, we see what could perhaps be described as something akin to God's first election broadcast. The story of Daniel contains examples of apocalyptic writing that were to prove extremely popular among the oppressed Jewish population for the next few hundred years. Presenting a picture of God's plans in a new way, God's unfolding manifesto was unpacked still further in vision rather than oracle, images rather than words.

Interpreting dreams for the ruling authorities, much as Joseph had done, Daniel communicated another political vision, but this time it related directly to the plans that God had in store for the government of the world. Daniel saw a succession of kingdoms that would occupy and rule. At the very end, however, the most startling prediction was made: God's kingdom, the one promised to David, would appear and would never be destroyed. Not only that, but it would bring an end to all the kingdoms that had gone before (Daniel 2:44).

# The bombshell

As an election campaign reaches its climax, it is not unheard-of for a political party to prepare a 'bombshell'. This is the term given to a measure that a party will keep secret till polling day. The bombshell can take the form of an action, an announcement or a revelation designed to convince wavering voters at the very last moment.

God's bombshell was just as mysterious as any ever produced by a political party. An enigmatic figure had for a long time been developing in the midst of the revelations and social comment of the prophets.

This figure took several different forms. Perhaps the most obvious was the idea of a Davidic king. With its roots in the covenant made to David, the theme was taken up by Isaiah, Jeremiah, Micah and Ezekiel. Isaiah prophesied that the king would bring peace to both Israel and the nations of the world. He would be a righteous judge who would slay the wicked and aid the poor (Isaiah 9:6–7; 11:1–10). In complete contrast was the figure of a suffering servant who would establish God's will through anguish and pain (Isaiah 42:1–4; 49:1–6; 50:4–9; 52:13; 53:12). Yet another concept developed in the inter-testamental literature—the 'Son of Man'. Perhaps a strange title to our ears, it was the natural Hebrew term for 'human being'. Finally, there was the 'eschatological prophet'— the closest we get to a messianic figure. Pictured as a prophet proclaiming good news, he was neither a Davidic king nor a suffering servant. His authority was in his anointing (Isaiah 1:1–4).

Quite how all these figures hung together was unclear to most people at the time. Not surprisingly, however, it was the idea of the Davidic king and the eschatological prophet that captured the public imagination. A significant number hoped for a Messiah who would be God's agent, in the long tradition of God's agents from Abraham onwards. The Messiah (or 'Christ') would set things right and help to establish God's kingdom.

# Election day

Election day finally arrived and at Bethlehem in Judea God's manifesto was finally revealed in all its fullness, in the form of Jesus Christ. At his birth Jesus was greeted as a king (Luke 1:32). Not surprisingly, this presented a significant threat to those who already held the political power. It was suggested that Jesus was to be a political leader. Persecution swiftly followed. A programme reminiscent of Pharaoh's population policy was launched to try to eliminate the potential threat, and Jesus' family fled to seek asylum in Egypt. There Jesus spent the first few years of his life in exile (Matthew 2:13–16).

The years passed and Jesus grew up until one day, in his home town of Nazareth, Jesus made the announcement that was to turn the world upside down. Striding to the front of what we might call his local council, he quoted from the prophecy of Isaiah:

*The spirit of the Lord is on me, because he has anointed me to preach good news to the poor. He has sent me to proclaim freedom for the prisoners and recovery of sight for the blind, to release the oppressed, to proclaim the year of the Lord's favour (Luke 4:18–19).*

But the crucial part was still to come. Sitting down, with the eyes of everyone in the synagogue fixed on him, Jesus put an end to the speculation about when the Messiah would come. 'Today,' said Jesus, 'this scripture is fulfilled in your hearing.'

In quoting from the messianic prophecy of Isaiah, Jesus declared that *he* was the anointed one. *He* was the politician that Israel had been waiting for all these years. *He* was the one who was bringing the new kingdom. This was a bombshell designed to leave no potential waverer in any doubt.

The rest of Jesus' ministry was devoted to explaining what this new kingdom would be. The vision was of a new social order where slaves would be freed, the sick healed and the poor liberated. But he didn't just talk about his vision of the future, he also showed what he meant in his actions, including healings, exorcisms and radical teaching.

But what Jesus was proclaiming was not all good news. In fact, it was downright bad news for the political establishment. Jesus told stories that singled out politicians who neglected their duty to care for those in distress (Luke 10:31–32). He encountered rich young rulers and told them to get rid of their wealth. He launched scathing attacks on the abuse of power by religious and political leaders (Matthew 23; Luke 6:24; 13:32).

While most political figures will do their best to keep away from disreputable company, Jesus did quite the reverse. He spent a great deal of time with known criminals, violent revolutionaries, sexual offenders and those guilty of corruption. In spite of this, his popular support grew, as he showed an authority that seemed to be lacking in the religious leaders—the same politicians who used the fact that he ate in disreputable company to try to smear him (Matthew 11:19; Luke 7:34).

The political classes also tried to catch Jesus out on a range of subjects. They asked him economic questions about the way the tax system was administered. They quizzed him about sexual ethics. Unable to catch him in their traps, they also tried to remove him permanently by claiming that he was filled with an evil spirit, blasphemous, and a false prophet (John 7:52; 8:4–8; 10:19–33), all of which qualified as capital offences under Jewish law.[2]

Aware of the implications of the message that he was bringing, Jesus warned his disciples that they would be handed over to the political authorities and would suffer. Undeterred, the disciples were resolute in their support. So committed were they to the cause that Jesus had to warn them about jockeying for political position (Mark 9:33–37; Matthew 18:1; Luke 9:46).

It was in the capital city of Jerusalem that Jesus' ministry reached its climax. Upon his arrival in the city of David, Jesus was greeted as the Davidic king. In line with the messianic expectation, he went to the temple, the centre of spiritual and civil authority.[3] Once there, however, his actions were somewhat different from what might have been expected. Overturning the tables of the money changers, he committed one more act of defiance against the political system (Matthew 21:12–13).

For a while now, several groups of opponents had been intent on killing Jesus (Matthew 12:14; Mark 3:6; Luke 13:31). It was at this point that the chief priests and teachers of the law joined them (Mark 11:18). A meeting of the supreme religious and political council (the Sanhedrin) was called and a coalition formed to take his life (John 11:46–53).

In exchange for money, Jesus was betrayed by one of his own followers. At Gethsemane, the high priest's soldiers arrested him. Brought before the high priest, Jesus faced a range of false accusations. The Sanhedrin could make none of them stick, however. Finally they asked him about his claim to be the Messiah. 'Yes, it is as you say,' replied Jesus (Matthew 26:64).

This was enough for the high priest, and the Jewish leaders took Jesus to the Roman governor, Pilate. There they brought accusations that Jesus was a revolutionary. Perhaps most notably, they accused him of telling people not to pay their taxes (Luke 23:2).

Pilate, however, could find nothing wrong. He therefore offered to release a prisoner, as was the custom at the Passover. He asked the people assembled to choose between the revolutionary Barabbas and Jesus. Manipulated by the very Jerusalem politicians who both oppressed them and also feared their insurrectionary potential, the crowd clamoured and voted against the one who, as far as they were concerned, had failed to deliver on God's promises (Matthew 27:20).

When the election finally came and the people were asked to vote, the manifesto in the form of Jesus Christ was rejected. The consequences, however, appeared more dire than in any normal election defeat.

Jesus was crucified and died. So the election was lost. Or was it?

It seems that there was one aspect of the political process that the Opposition had misunderstood. The opponents of God's manifesto had taken it for granted that power and authority depended upon popularity. But what if it wasn't the voters who were going to have the final say? What if success didn't depend upon acceptance or rejection by the electorate?

While to an outsider it might seem that God's manifesto had been defeated, in the end the opposite was true. In one final demonstration that silenced the Opposition once and for all, Jesus proved that, far from being defeated, he had in fact won.

On the third day, Jesus rose from the dead, proving that it was he who had the authority once again.

## NOTES

1   For more discussion of Nimrod, see Bauckham, *The Bible in Politics*, p. 11 and
    C. Westermann, *Genesis 1—11: A Commentary* (SPCK, 1984), pp. 514–518

2   For more details see V.W. Redekop, *A Life for a Life: the Death Penalty on Trial* (Herald Press, 1990), p. 49

3   C. Marshall, *Kingdom Come: The Kingdom of God in the Teaching of Jesus* (Impetus Publications, 1990), p. 78

# Chapter 3

# What's the Big Idea?

The 'vision thing'—the big idea that's going to hold everything together—is something that politicians cannot afford to be without. It is the driving force behind every great manifesto. At election time and, to a lesser extent, between elections, thousands of column inches are devoted to discussing it, explaining it and dissecting it. It gives the purpose, direction and goal of the electoral process. It is the picture that captures the political imagination.

Chapter 2 took us on a whistle-stop tour of salvation history. It was not, of course, a comprehensive or definitive account of the people of God. There were many gaps—it finished with Jesus' death, and did not go on to talk about his resurrection, ascension or the early Church, which we will come to discuss later. It also emphasized just one particular dimension of the unfolding of God's purposes. It drew comparisons between events of thousands of years ago and political events today that will, I am sure, make some theologians extremely uncomfortable, if not cause them to hop up and down anxiously.

Relating the salvation story in this way, for all its pitfalls, does serve a purpose. It gives us the big picture—it sets out God's vision. It allows us to stand back and reflect upon the painting that God has created upon the canvas of the time. This is no quick political sketch. It depicts in broad strokes what God has been up to all these years since the world was created.

At the 2001 general election, Tony Blair, in his first keynote speech of the campaign at his constituency in Sedgfield, set out his own vision.

*There is much talk in politics of the need for a big idea. New Labour's big idea is the development of human potential, the belief that there is talent and ability and caring in each individual that often lies unnurtured or discouraged. Our ideology is the development of the human mind to its fullest natural extent, building national strength and prosperity by tapping the potential of all the people. It is based on a notion of equality that is not about outcomes or incomes; but about equal worth. It is what has driven me all my political life.*[1]

In some respects, Blair was on to something. God's vision is that the harmony and goodness of creation should be restored. Despite the violence and oppression, inequality, selfishness and injustice that resulted from the Fall, things will once again be made right. Even the wolf will lie down with the lamb (Isaiah 11:6–9). Eventually, human beings will become fully human again, reflecting the image of their creator. All things will be reconciled under one head (Ephesians 1:10).

The plan, of course, was not always clear for all to see. We saw throughout the last chapter how God's purposes were revealed bit by bit. The apostle Paul points out that God's agenda was kept secret for many years. It was a mystery. Like the most closely guarded official secret, God's manifesto included a divine purpose that God had designed from eternity but had kept hidden from people until the appointed time (Romans 16:25; Ephesians 3:9; Colossians 1:26).

As time went on, God's campaign unfolded. God revealed a little more detail about how the vision was to be fulfilled. But it was only in the life, death and resurrection of Jesus Christ—God's manifesto incarnate—that the full implications of God's agenda were made clear.

When we sit back and reflect on the unfolding events, what we find is that God's vision for the world has always been much more than a spiritual one. In fact, God's vision has been political in all three senses of the word that we outlined in the first chapter.

# A new social order

First, God's purposes are by no means other-worldly. They are positively earthy. God cares about the stuff of everyday life. The plan is not that we should be rescued and whisked off to heaven from a planet that will one day be destroyed. Rather, it is that in the fullness of God's time all things will be restored to the way that they were in the beginning. Everything will be put right. The vision is, and always has been, of a new heaven *and a new earth* (2 Peter 3:13).

Jesus' death on the cross underlines this fact. It was a bloody, painful, political death—a death in which Jesus identified completely with the human condition. But his resurrection makes it clear that our hope lies in a redeemed creation. Jesus did not appear as some sort of ghost moving between earth and the afterlife. Rather he appeared in a new body, a real body, one that gives us hope that all things can be made right again.

This will come as quite a shock to many people. How often do we hear our ministers, vicars or pastors tell us from the front of the church that we are all off to heaven? The reality is rather different. We aren't going anywhere. Eternity starts here and now with the world that God has made and will one day restore to all its glory.

Jesus promised a new social order where slaves would be freed, the sick healed and the poor liberated. Justice and righteousness would be the hallmarks of this new age, where things would be made right once and for all. The violence that had entered the creation would once again be replaced by peace, and all those suffering oppression, whether physical or spiritual, would finally experience true release.

As we saw in the first chapter, in our privatized faith we have a tendency to interpret what Jesus did in purely spiritual terms. We talk of 'spiritual freedom' and 'peace in our souls'. We should not belittle what it means to experience spiritual release, but to stop there is to short-change what Jesus both said and did. In line with

God's vision of a redeemed creation, it was salvation of the physical as well as the spiritual that Jesus brought.

Jesus did not speculate about the nature of human society in the manner of a Greek philosopher, or lay out a set of policy prescriptions, as our own politicians do. Had he done so, it would not have been long before what he said was obsolete and irrelevant. But the new kingdom that he described does have some surprisingly specific social and political implications. Jesus' declaration in the synagogue at Nazareth alone (Luke 4:18–19) contains a radical strategy for social renewal:

*The spirit of the Lord is on me, because he has anointed me to preach good news to the poor. He has sent me to proclaim freedom for the prisoners, and recovery of sight for the blind, to release the oppressed, to proclaim the year of the Lord's favour.*

This is not just release from spiritual poverty, blindness and oppression. To prove it, Jesus went on to do everything contained in that passage. There was indeed good news for the poor, sight for the blind, release for the oppressed. Even Barabbas the prisoner was set free.

In so doing, Jesus demonstrated that the new social order was already here. The time had come for the vision to be put in place. The manifesto was to be implemented. Everywhere were the signs —healings and exorcisms, feeding miracles, fellowship over meals with the excluded and forgiveness of sins.

## A new authority

A new social order was by no means all that God's vision entailed. In the second sense of the word 'political' it should now be clear that the salvation story is all about what lies at the heart of politics, and what drives so many political people—power and authority.

God's original purpose was not to hold on to all the power, or even to give authority over the creation to a select few. It was that power and authority should be held by all humankind. Our authority, however, was lost in the Fall. God's unfolding agenda has been the plan to restore that authority once and for all. It was always God's purpose that authority over the creation should rest with those made in God's image—and God's purposes are always fulfilled. God's manifesto involves the restoration of that image.

Through the new kingdom, God's power and authority were being re-established—and established in the way that God had always intended. God's gentle rule broke into the world once again in the way that it had originally been given to humankind. Through another radical devolution of power it was another free gift, simply because God loved the world he created. It even meant great personal cost— Christ's suffering and death—in the same way that God had seen his own rejection in the Fall. God's manifesto was consistent from start to finish.

Although God's agenda often unfolded in political contexts, it is clear that the answer to the world's problems was not going to come in the form of traditional politics. No king, no ruler, no earthly power, however good, was ever going to be able to restore the authority over the created order. Kings can do justice and they can steward the creation, but they have no power to deal with the root of the problem —the sin, the fundamental rebellion against God's rule. All have sinned, and in their helplessness have lost the authority that God gave.

For those who had eyes to see, it was always clear that authority rested with God rather than political office. It was Moses, not Pharaoh; the judges, not the kings of Israel; Samuel, not Saul, who held the real authority.

It was only through the mystery of the cross that the authority was finally restored and the power of sin and death was broken. Then the relationship between God and humankind was made right again. The atonement was exactly that—an 'at-one-ment'. Enemies were brought into peace and friendship; the creation was reconciled with the creator. In the words of the apostle Paul, 'We have peace with God through our Lord Jesus Christ' (Romans 5:1).

*But now in Christ Jesus you who once were far off have been brought near by the blood of Christ. For he is our peace; in his flesh he has made both groups into one... So he came and proclaimed peace to you who were far off and peace to those who were near; for through him both of us have access in one Spirit to the Father (Ephesians 2:13–18).*

It is the resurrection that is the final proof of the new authority—which extends even to power over death.

## A new politics

Finally, there should be little doubt when we look at the salvation story that God has always been involved right at the heart of politics—and in that sense his purposes are political too. The salvation story is frequently an account of how the people of God have operated in and around politics, both as a nation—a political entity—and in other ways as well. It should also be clear, however, that God's politics differs in very important ways from the politics that we see on our televisions and read about in our newspapers every day.

Jesus did not march in as a warrior king and impose the new reign of justice and righteousness that many people were waiting for. Nor did he fulfil the nationalistic expectation that God's people would be handed the political power. Rather, he showed something far more subtle, far more beautiful and far more perfect. In both his life and death he showed that the new kingdom had an entirely new set of values. This was not a kingdom of domination and control. It was a kingdom of sacrifice and service.

A common mistake is to conclude from this that Jesus was not political, but Jesus demonstrated instead a new type of politics. In place of the violence and control that most political systems display, Jesus brought peace and freedom. Instead of battles for power, Jesus presented a new way of powerlessness.

As with the new authority, it is the cross that is at the centre of the new politics. It is the cross that epitomizes what the new politics is about. Rather than taking the power for ourselves, it is about laying down our own interests and giving up power for the sake of others. But we do not do so without hope, for we know that the cross is not the end. While it may seem like political failure to lay down the power and put our self-interest last, we know that the final result will be life. Indeed, it is only the new politics that has the power to bring resurrection life.

## The political tension

So radical and unexpected was this new kingdom that even those closest to Jesus had a hard time understanding it.

We too can easily miss it. You could be forgiven for wondering even now whether the new kingdom was anything more than a pipe-dream. A quick look around us reveals that the vision may be a long way from being realized. The wars, the famines, the violence and the inequality seem to be just as present as they ever were. Where is the political vision that Jesus talked about? After all the twists and turns of salvation history, has anything really changed? Has God's rule really been re-established?

The answer is 'yes' but also 'no'. The answer is 'yes' because God's manifesto—the plan to bring God's vision to completion—has broken into our world in the form of Jesus Christ and the new kingdom. The plan has been revealed and is being put into action. Jesus has reconciled us to God. He has also shown us a new way of living, a new way of being, which involves new values and a new kingdom. But more than that, he has given us the opportunity to taste and experience the new heaven and the new earth that are coming, living as citizens of that kingdom right now (Ephesians 2:19; Philippians 3:20). We have had the authority of God, which was lost in the Fall, restored to us.

But the answer is also 'no'. God has also made it clear that only on the great day when Jesus returns will the vision be experienced in all its fullness. God's kingdom may have broken in, but we await its final consummation. Things will still go wrong. There will still be injustice, inequality and pain all around us. We cannot build God's kingdom ourselves—that is God's job. One day, we are told, the king will return, and when he does, the new heaven and a new earth will finally be established (2 Peter 3:13). Then God's manifesto will reach its fulfilment.

So we find ourselves right in the middle of a 'yes and no' tension—a 'now but not yet' with regard to God's political agenda. On the one hand, God's authority has broken in once again in the form of the new kingdom. On the other, we await the final consummation of that kingdom, on the day when Jesus returns.

So where does that leave us? In light of this most amazing of stories, where do we fit into this paradoxical situation?

## God's spin doctors

We all know well the last words of Jesus before he ascended into heaven: 'Go into all the world and preach the good news to all creation' (Mark 16:15). The words of the great commission trip easily off our lips. Perhaps rarely do we stop to consider, though, what a radical message this really is.

Picture the scene. You are a servant, standing on the battlements of a first-century fortress. The sun beats down on your head as you try to glare through the beads of sweat that trickle into your eyes, at the speck on the horizon coming towards you. In the distance you think you can see the messenger returning from the battle. He will tell you whether your people are to serve a foreign king, or whether your own king has been victorious. In his person lies the news that you are to be oppressed and subject to a foreign power for years to come, or the news that your future is safe in the hands of your king who has triumphed. Will he bring news of a new age of peace and prosperity, or violence and poverty?

The word *evangel*, used by the New Testament writers to mean 'gospel' or 'good news', had an important political significance.[2] It was not just an ordinary term to describe the reporting of glad tidings; it was the word used by just such a messenger returning from a battle to report a victory to kings. It was the news that the political climate had changed, and that a new regime was in place. It was a profoundly political message—in all three senses of the word.

In the same way, our own *evangel* has at its heart a political message—that God's rule has been re-established. The battle has been won. The authority that was lost in creation has been restored to humankind. Creation is being freed from its bondage to sin, and God's government is being put back in place. All things are being made right again.

This is good news indeed, and this is the news that we find ourselves possessing as we live in the now-but-not-yet tension, but it is also news that needs to be communicated. We are like that messenger, returning from the battle with news that the whole world is changing. A new political age is here.

You have probably never thought of yourself as a 'spin doctor'— one of those shadowy figures whom you can never quite identify, but who you know lurk behind the news. Spin doctors have got quite a bad reputation over the last few years. They are seen by most as people who distort, twist or exaggerate the truth—usually for some kind of political gain.

Originally, however, the job of spin doctors was to communicate truthfully and accurately the messages that their employers wished them to get across. Like a messenger returning from battle two thousand years ago, they carried the authority of a political leader on whose behalf they spoke. They were, in effect, witnesses to the actions and words of the people they represented.

Perhaps the image of a spin doctor is even more helpful in that their job is not simply to report the news and hope that their message gets across. Rather, spin doctors make sure that their story is reported as it competes with the thousands of other voices for the attention of the public. They make certain that their particular political agenda gets the highest billing possible.

As unpalatable as it may seem, Jesus empowered the disciples to be his spin doctors. Early on in his ministry, Jesus sent out the disciples with a message: 'As you go, preach this message: "The kingdom of heaven is near." Heal the sick, raise the dead, cleanse those who have leprosy, drive out demons' (Matthew 10:7–8).

The disciples did not wait for people to come to them. They were given authority and told to go out and ensure that God's political agenda was made known.

It is hard for us to imagine what it must have been like for people to hear the radical political message as the disciples came proclaiming the news of the new kingdom. Rarely do we have a similar experience in our depoliticized culture. The closest we come is probably at election time when we wait for that dreaded knock at the door from the party activists and canvassers. Each has their own message and set of promises about what their candidate can do for us. But have you ever wondered what would happen if you asked them to show you? What would they do if, having told you that hospital waiting lists would be shorter, or class sizes would be smaller, you said, 'OK, then—prove it!'

Unlike any spin doctor or party hack, the disciples didn't come with an empty message. As the disciples travelled from town to town, those who encountered them were told the good news of the kingdom—and the disciples were able to prove it. The news was backed up with action. The good news was release for the captives, sight for the blind, health for the sick. All the consequences of the fallen creation were going to be reversed, and to show them that this wasn't empty rhetoric, the work started then and there. The sick were made well, the dead were raised, and demons were driven out.

Those who encountered the disciples didn't just hear about the kingdom of God. They came near the kingdom of God, and experienced the kingdom breaking in for themselves. God's vision was beginning to take place before their eyes. No wonder the message was so powerful!

# Political empowerment

Like the disciples, Jesus calls us to proclaim the good news of his kingdom in both word and deed to all of creation. This is what the great commission means. Through both our speech and actions, we are to show that God's new order of justice is here, that God's authority is being established and all things are being made right again.

Jesus, however, also made clear that we were not going to have to go out and do all this on our own. The Holy Spirit was to come and lead us into all truth (John 14:15–27; 16:13).

It is a staggering thought that when we receive the Holy Spirit, we are also once again politically empowered. We are used to thinking of power as something that comes from controlling multi-national corporations, large media empires or high political office. God shows, however, that there is a power more real. God's definition of power and authority is not about control—being able to get people to do what you want, or making things go your way. Rather, it is about being in harmony with the character of God. True authority comes from being restored to the way we were in creation—made in the image of God. Those who come into harmony with God's character are the ones with the real power.

Jesus told the disciples that they would receive this power when the Holy Spirit came (Acts 1:8). It is the Holy Spirit who enables us to enter into the reality of the new kingdom. It is the Holy Spirit who enables us to come into harmony with God's character and gives us the authority to be God's agents in creation once again.

That is an amazing thing to say, but one that is vital to grasp. Through the Holy Spirit we are once again political beings, carrying God's authority. Through the Holy Spirit we take our places in the salvation story. We now become God's agents, making all things right again. It is part of our job now to stand against the effects of the Fall, to stand for justice and peace, to protect the vulnerable—to bring God's authority to the creation. This is not some 'liberal' or 'social' gospel. It is *the* gospel!

When it comes to Christian campaigning, it is not unusual to hear people talk about 'Christian issues'. 'Marriage', for example, is often quoted as a Christian issue that churches should be actively campaigning about. On the other hand, something like 'constitutional reform' or 'the single currency' are not seen in quite the same terms. But the fact that we are to take our position as agents of the creation once again makes it clear that there can no longer be any sacred–secular divide. We have a responsibility for everything. The whole earth belongs to God, and we are to take our places in looking after it. Nor is this only for those involved in public life. Whatever our jobs, whether we are doctors, writers, musicians or street cleaners, we are doing our work as God's agents in creation. Our work is Christian work. It is part of following Jesus.

Our work is also political in another sense, because by doing it we are demonstrating God's new authority over the creation. Our work, our lives, are political acts. Both the way that we do our work and our reasons for doing it are a political statement and a witness to the gospel—the good news.

We saw in the last chapter that God's intention was for his people to be a light to the nations. Israel was to be distinctive, a model for a new way of living with a new set of values. This aspiration didn't end with Jesus. The first thing that Jesus did was to convene a discipleship community. The kingdom involved the calling together of a new society, citizens of the new kingdom, to live according to the standards of the new age that was to come. This community was to be a witness to God's new social order in its actions as well as its words.

It is no coincidence that at Pentecost, when the Holy Spirit empowered the new community, they pooled all their possessions together, ate together and gave to all who had need. What else could they do? It was the natural witness and outworking of the gospel message—the good news of the kingdom of God.

This task now falls to us too.

## Your mission, should you accept it...

The early Church was not to have an easy time of it. Perhaps this should have come as no surprise, for Jesus had never led them to believe anything else. Even before his death, when Jesus despatched his disciples on their mission he did so with a warning: 'Be on your guard against men; they will hand you over to the local councils and flog you in their synagogues. On my account you will be brought before governors and kings as witnesses to them and to the Gentiles' (Matthew 10:17–18).

Why was this? Surely, if they were going out to give everyone such good news, it would be odd indeed to shoot the messenger?

The fact is, however, that the message was not good news for everyone. The news that a new kingdom is breaking in is not particularly glad tidings if you are in charge of the old kingdom. The disciples' mission was thoroughly subversive as far as the old order was concerned.

Ask the average Christian which film star they most closely identify with in their spiritual journey, and you can be pretty sure that it won't be Tom Cruise or Pierce Brosnan. While we talk a great deal of 'mission', if we're honest with ourselves we will admit that the word is more likely to conjure up images of guitar-strumming street evangelists than a subversive agent like James Bond or Ethan Hunt. Most of us aren't really sure what our mission is, so we can hardly make a choice about whether or not to accept it.

Mission is a central part of what it means to be a Christian. It is our response to what has been revealed about God, God's plans and purposes, in the salvation story. Indeed, our mission is to take our own places within that amazing story.

As we shall see in the next chapter, like the heroes in the Hollywood blockbusters our own mission—should we choose to accept it—is one that will rock the world of the powerful and turn the world upside down.

The vision that Jesus brought was one of reconciliation, peace and love; but at the same time it was one of conflict, of challenge, of confrontation. 'I did not come to bring peace, but a sword,' Jesus warned (Matthew 10:34).

## NOTES

1   Tony Blair, Prime Minister and Leader of the Labour Party, adoption speech to Sedgefield Labour Party members, 13 May 2001
2   J.H. Yoder, *The Politics of Jesus* (Eerdmans and The Paternoster Press, 1994), p. 28

# Chapter 4

# Knowing the Opposition

'Fly the flag, Mr Bartley' ran the headline in the Christian newspaper. I was quite taken aback because, to my knowledge, the
weekly had never printed any reader's letter as an article before—
but here it was in black and white. Someone had sent a letter to the
editor and they had decided to print it as a full-blown story with a
big headline containing my name. I was certainly not accustomed
to receiving such individual attention.

The reason for the special treatment was a piece that I had
written as my regular column two weeks before. I had suggested
that the debate over the age of consent for homosexual sex might
not be as black-and-white as many evangelicals thought that it was.
There were two sides to every debate, and it was my opinion that
we needed to be careful about how we approached the subject.

The result was a flood of e-mails, letters and phone calls from
people who were deeply upset by what I had written. Even the
newspaper seemed to have joined in!

The main point made by both the newspaper article and the
many people who contacted me was that I was letting the side
down by not coming out (if you will excuse the pun) and con-
demning outright the Government's plans to equalize the ages
of consent for homosexual and heterosexual sex. My article was
somehow seen as a betrayal, an own goal in the battle between 'us'
and 'them'. In short, I had let the side down. I was not 'flying the
flag'.

We have developed our own language of what we consider to
be 'sound' and 'unsound'. We love to draw distinctions between

'our side' and 'their side'. I have lost count of the number of times I have heard Christians talking about the 'secularists', with their 'humanist' values, 'politically correct' or 'liberal' agenda. Whether it be 'evangelical', 'conservative' or 'pro-life', there seems to be no end to the labels around which we ourselves rally, forming groupings either mentally or literally.

Christians are, of course, far from being alone when it comes to dividing the world into opposing camps. 'Are they one of us?' was Margaret Thatcher's famous cry when she applied her political litmus test. For her, people were either in the Right camp or the wrong camp.

There is a need to name and identify specific beliefs, positions and opinions, but this kind of language can all too easily lead us down an unhelpful road. A group soon becomes singled out as something to be battled against and defeated. This does no justice to the depth and complexity of debate. It polarizes the positions. But perhaps most seriously, it misses the point about whom our struggle is really against. Who, after all, is the real opponent of God's political agenda?

## Engaging the powers

*For our struggle is not against flesh and blood, but against the rulers, against the authorities, against the powers of this dark world and against the spiritual forces of evil in the heavenly realms (Ephesians 6:12).*

In charismatic circles, that verse from Ephesians is generally accompanied by a lot of chorus-singing and fervent prayer as people 'do some spiritual warfare' and 'tear down the strongholds'. But these powers and principalities are not something 'out there' just to be prayed and sung against. They are very real, very tangible, and manifest in very formidable ways. The powers exist, quite simply, wherever there is power. In local councils, families, schools, churches or workplaces, there the powers will be. The powers were part of the created order, and, like the rest of creation, are fallen and in need of redemption.

It is often hard for us to appreciate in our materialistic Western world that an institution might have a 'spirituality', but behind every grouping and organization—political or otherwise—there is a power. This is the way that God made the world to work. Each power has both heavenly and earthly, spiritual and institutional manifestations. Perhaps a 'corporate culture' might be the closest that we ever come to expressing it.

As I have already mentioned, for a brief period after I left school I worked abroad for a missionary organization. During that time, with a small group of people from around the world I found myself on a remote Pacific island helping to run a children's holiday club.

We were all staying in a small church there, the women in the actual church building and the men in a small outbuilding nearby. A few hours after we had settled in, some of us—myself included—began to experience a deep fear. There was no apparent reason for it. There was nothing to be scared of. It was not particularly rational, but fear it was, nevertheless. When we left the place, the fear went away; and when we returned the fear returned too.

To this day I have not been able to explain the experience, but whether abroad or in our own countries many of us have had times when we have walked into buildings, or perhaps areas of a town, and felt perhaps a lightness or a feeling of oppression and despondency.

Visitors to Nazi Germany and South Africa under the apartheid system spoke of the sense of evil 'in the air' and their relief at leaving. There is often a distinctive atmosphere as you walk into a football stadium. Many people remarked on a notable difference across the UK the day after the 1997 election, when Tony Blair was elected, or indeed when the Princess of Wales died.

It is all too easy to mistake the feelings that we have for the presence of the powers, and we must be very careful to discern what the powers are, but what I am suggesting is that we have all experienced the presence of the powers in many situations, while perhaps not always acknowledging that there are fundamental spiritual realities underlying the political, social and economic systems.

As Christians, our struggle is with these powers first and foremost. We do not battle against people, parties or institutions. It is not the government, the 'secularists' or a political lobby that we are seeking to defeat. Our real struggles are more far-reaching and profound.

# Partisanship

When I graduated from university, my first job was as a researcher to an MP. I had no political affiliation, but since the Conservative party was in government I decided that it would be good experience to go and work for a Tory Member of Parliament.

As anyone who has worked in Parliament will know, the values of the political parties are quite different from the values of most academic institutions. At university, you are taught to weigh up all sides of a debate, listen to the arguments and look for the truth in a situation, but as a parliamentary researcher, the situation is by no means the same. The research that you are asked to undertake usually involves creating strong arguments to bolster your political position. Frequently this means simultaneously undermining the arguments of your opponents, regardless of their merit.

My first trip to the party Whips' office—the place where the party managers are based—came as a huge shock. There, a whole selection of typed briefs are available for the debates that are coming up in the House of Commons. Instead of reasoned arguments, however, they generally contain a series of carefully constructed points to provide political ammunition with which to undermine the arguments of your opponents and to talk up your own party's ideas and policies. Getting at the truth is not really the point.

Each brief, usually put together by the Party's central office, would be divided into several sections. One section might list the party's 'successes'. The next would perhaps list the opposition's 'failures'. Another will list why the other parties' proposals won't work and so on. There is no balance whatsoever. Each document is designed simply to provide as much ammunition as possible to defeat the 'enemy'—whichever party that may be.

It has never ceased to amaze me that many people working in the field of politics—including many who profess a Christian faith— don't see this as a problem. It is, after all, the way that politics works, and if you want to be involved, they say, this is the way that you will have to behave. Such arguments completely fail to recognize the spiritual realities that lie beneath.

My own experience was that after just a few months of working in such an environment I began to take on the same approach myself. I took on wholeheartedly the arguments and values of the party for which I worked. By the end of the year, my perspective had completely changed. The more I worked within the context of a party, the more I took on the values of that system, to the point of defending it vigorously at all opportunities.

The powers are strong, and more often than not, when we join a group or institution the powers get a hold over us. We develop a natural bias toward the group. We see the group as right, and the others as wrong. It happens with nations, classes, football clubs and even churches, and the deeper into the institution that you get, the greater the hold that the powers exert.

A few years after I had begun my work in Parliament, I found myself working for the then Prime Minister, John Major, as part of his campaign team in the Conservative party leadership election against John Redwood. There the party spirit was at its height, but this time not around the party as a whole, but around the candidate whom we were supporting within the party.

The extent of the partisanship that pervaded the team could be seen in the internal briefings that would be issued to the campaign team every morning. The briefings were designed to equip people to deal with media enquiries, and to ensure that everyone was singing from the same political hymn sheet. Documents with such titles as 'Lines to take on Redwood' contained detailed points that MPs supporting John Major were supposed to use to undermine

John Redwood's campaign. They were little more than propaganda.

The absurdity was highlighted by one briefing that began with the words, 'There is nothing of substance from John Redwood today.' This was in a brief that was written before midday, long before John Redwood had made any statements that could be judged to be of substance or otherwise!

Outside the context of politics, the whole thing is seen for what it is—ridiculous in the extreme. But for those engaged at the political coal-face—those who are actively involved in political parties—it is a very serious and very important part of the political process. The party is there to win a battle against their opponents, and they will use all reasonable means at their disposal to do it.

Every now and then, however, there has been a political figure who has refused to give in to the system. William Wilberforce (1759–1833), the tireless campaigner against the slave trade, 'had a gift... for exploring both sides of a question' we are told by his biographer John Pollock. It was Wilberforce's desire that 'freedom of opinion would be restored and Party connections in a great measure vanish'.[1]

The apostle Paul, too, was unequivocal that we 'do not wage war as the world does' (2 Corinthians 10:3). He was equally emphatic in his views on 'party spirit'. Writing to the church at Galatia, he ranked it right alongside immorality, sorcery and idolatry (Galatians 5:19–21), and quite rightly so. This kind of behaviour is not just undesirable, it is anti-Christian. We should be under no illusions: party spirit works against truth and all that is good. As we shall see, it stands in complete opposition to the message of the gospel, and our mission is to challenge it.

# A different world

Involved in a campaign to encourage democracy in the area where I live, I once wrote to 150 local churches asking them whether they would support proposals to change the way that our local council was run. The powers of the mayor were being increased significantly under new government legislation. The group that I was working with asked whether churches wanted to see the council becoming more open and accountable in its decision-making, in light of the new powers of the mayor.

Out of 150 churches, I received replies from only six. One read as follows:

*Rarely does the name of the Mayor mean anything to us… when we elect (our local councillors) we trust that they know the personal qualities and political views of the mayor they elect, and they are in the best position to make the decision.*

Rather than challenging the way that our political systems operate, the response of many Christians has been to withdraw completely and hope for the best. Institutions and powers, particularly when it comes to politics, are often seen as a different world, one to be left well alone. There are politicians 'out there' who can do the job adequately. We have more important things to be getting on with.

Part of the reason for this state of affairs undoubtedly lies with our concept of 'the world'. When we recall the words in Ephesians about our battle against the powers, we think, in the words of the well-worn phrase, that we are to be 'in the world but not of it'. 'The world' is viewed as something that will taint us and make us less holy if we get too close to it.

When the line is drawn between 'us' and 'them', sacred and secular, the church and the world, politics is usually placed well over on the other side from where we stand. Politics is seen as something particularly 'worldly'. It is about compromise, and about issues and agendas that we do not consider to have much relevance to our faith. Churches are quite happy to leave their local councillors or MPs to get on with the job.

But is this what being 'in the world, but not of the world' really means? The theologian Walter Wink has suggested that it isn't. The Greek word *kosmos*, frequently translated in the New Testament as 'world', is much better translated as 'system'. When the New Testament talks of the 'world' in this way, it means not the creation but 'the human sociological realm that exists in estrangement from God'.[2] This realm or 'system' represents the dominant values in our society. It is the way that the world works. It is the procedures and methods by which most of our communities and workplaces operate.

Being 'in the world but not of the world' does not mean leaving the structures of our day, political or otherwise, well alone. Quite the reverse, in fact; it means that we are to live by a new set of values that challenge those structures. We are to engage with them fully. Whether it be in the local council or school, national politics or our workplace, we do not have an option to withdraw. Our values must, by definition, challenge the world around us, because they are God's values.

## It's the system, man

I wonder if you have ever stopped to analyse the dominant story or values that underlie most films on TV or at the cinema, in our books or in our children's tales?

Our stories generally go something like this. A group of goodies are being oppressed by baddies. A hero arrives, who is to be the liberator of the good guys and must save them. The hero helps the goodies to take up arms, or use justifiable violence to defeat the baddies and achieve salvation. The goodies then live happily ever after.

This is the theme of most cowboy Westerns. It is the underlying plot of most of the great film blockbusters. It is the stuff of most fairytales.

Now compare this story with the gospel story. Israel is a nation oppressed by the Romans, suffering injustice and hardship. Along comes the hero, Jesus, in whom not just Israel's hopes, but the hopes of the whole world rest. The hero promises liberation for the captives, justice for the downtrodden and a new kingdom of righteousness.

But here is where the story is radically different. Instead of embracing violent conquest and domination as many of his contemporaries expected, Jesus challenges the 'baddies' and 'goodies' alike. He even redefines who is a goody and a baddy, shattering the distinctions that the people had made between 'us' and 'them'. Then instead of taking up arms he lays down his own life, and is killed by the very oppressive system from which people were hoping to be freed. But then, through his death and resurrection, salvation comes not just for the 'goodies' but the 'baddies' as well.

Walter Wink calls the first story 'the myth of redemptive violence'. It has its roots in a great Babylonian myth, and highlights the system on which so much of our society and perhaps culture is based. It is found in many of the great stories of history but also in our politics, our business dealings, our judicial system—pretty much everywhere. It is the lie that by somehow dominating your opponent you can bring salvation, or at least a good society.

One of the images that will stick in most people's minds from the 2001 general election campaign is the punch that was thrown by the then Deputy Prime Minister. A protestor hurled an egg, and John Prescott's response—whether it was reflex or otherwise—was to turn round with a quick left hook that hit the protestor squarely on the jaw.

What Mr Prescott did was little more than an outward manifestation of the values upon which our political system is based. Every week at Prime Minister's Question Time, the party leaders attempt to get the better of each other by attacking the other, making fun, and trying to gain the upper hand. The primary concern of each one is to beat their opponents. The aim is to dominate and defeat the other side by all means possible. The next day, their performance will be evaluated in the press according to who scored most points or perhaps who boosted the morale of the MPs sitting behind them.

When challenged about this, the politicians will readily admit it.

In fact, it is frequently claimed that this is the way a healthy democracy should operate. The justification is offered that if both sides go at each other as hard as they can, somehow the result will be fair and the best for all concerned. It is claimed that we need an effective opposition to hold the Government to account. By opposing everything that the Government does, an opposition, it is suggested, will expose the flaws, problems or even corruption of the state.

The system is, of course, far from unique to our politics. The values are similar to the trial-by-combat of medieval times. Two knights rode at each other, lances at the ready, trying to destroy the other. The righteous one, it was supposed, would be the one who could dominate the other and win. These are the values that underlie the free market as businesses seek to dominate one another to gain market share. The strongest and most healthy survive. In our legal system, the prosecution and the defence try to win their case by dominating each other. In each context it is argued that the best outcomes will result, and that this is the system by which our lives should be run and ordered.

This is the system that we are up against as Christians. This is the kind of 'world' that we are to challenge. This is the kind of world we are to be in—but not of. It is based on a lie and stands in total contrast to the values of the new kingdom that Jesus brought and taught. It stands in complete contradiction to the good news of the gospel story to which we must witness.

## So we're part of the system too?

Our job, then, is to engage with the powers that lie behind these systems, with the gospel message that has at its heart the cross of Christ. Earlier it was mentioned that 'the powers' exist in what might be called secular environments such as local councils, schools and families. It was also hinted that the powers exist in religious contexts too.

For several years now, I have been working with Christians who are involved in politics, from the people who run Christian pressure groups to Parliamentarians. Many of us meet regularly to pray, to share ideas and information. One theme continually dominates the discussions at such meetings. The people present are intensely discouraged. They feel as if they are fighting a losing battle. They see what they will term a 'moral slide' or a 'secularist' agenda and believe that it is their job to do all they can to stop it.

The solution frequently offered is that we need a new political force that unites Christians into one great power block. Whether it is to be a political party, a large coalition or an alliance, the thinking is that if only we were a power to be reckoned with, we could really make a difference. It is a mantra that is repeated in many different contexts. I have been present at meeting after meeting over the last ten years where the agenda has been to discuss what shape this force might take, and how it should come together.

By taking up such an agenda, however, the people of God are unwittingly adopting the values of the domination system. Rather than challenging the powers, they are siding with them—in fact, supporting the very system that we are supposed to be battling against. We are waging war with the world's weapons, not God's weapons—the opposite of the apostle Paul's advice two thousand years ago (2 Corinthians 10:4).

This is a trap that the people of God have fallen into again and again. According to John's Gospel, this is what Jesus said at his trial: 'I have spoken openly to the world (*kosmos*)... I always taught in the synagogue or at the temple' (John 18:20). Here, Jesus equated the world (*kosmos*) with the religious institutions of his day. In modern-day terms, the world was not something beyond the doors of the church, it *was* the church! Why is this? In the words of Walter Wink, Jesus is referring to a 'religious system that, as the author portrays it, is unaware of its alienation from God'.[3] As we saw in Chapter 2, the people of God did not understand the way in which the new kingdom would come. They operated under a different system that was not in tune with God's political agenda.

Could it be that the Church is similarly unaware of its alienation from God? Could it be that we are now doing exactly the same as the religious powers of Jesus' day? Rather than being a subversive force in challenging the domination system, have we in fact taken the domination system as our own?

# The good, the bad and the ugly

A monochrome advert by a well-known Christian pressure group stated the following: 'This advert is black and white… so are the issues'. Rarely, however, is this statement true. More often than not, the issues that we deal with are extremely complex and we need to tread most carefully. In every political position there is good and there is bad. In every issue there is truth and there are lies. It is not our job to defeat everyone who holds a contrary position to our own. It is our job to expose both the good and the bad, the truth and the lies, in every political situation.

'Secularization', for example, was singled out by one Christian organization as a force to be fought at a recent general election. It certainly tends to carry negative connotations, but secularization can be a force for good as well as bad. It was the forces of secularization in the 18th-century intellectual movement of the Enlightenment that brought religious liberty, and ended centuries of persecution by the Catholic and then the Protestant Church, against religious dissent in Europe. Jesus himself was a secularizing force against the religion that tied people up in spiritual knots.

When we see the 'secularists', or this or that 'lobby', as an enemy to be defeated, the danger is that we see them as all bad. As in the myth of redemptive violence, we make them our enemy—and see our mission as to defeat and dominate them. But in so doing we may well be putting ourselves in opposition to God's truth.

I began this chapter by mentioning an article that I had written about the age of consent for homosexual sex. The way in which Christians have campaigned on issues of sexuality is a very good illustration of the way they have collaborated with the domination system.

Christians have for many years been at the forefront of campaigning against the introduction of 'same-sex partnerships'. The main point made by Christian campaigners is that by giving legal status to same-sex couples, the institution of marriage will somehow be undermined.

The first thing to notice about this kind of campaign is that the political landscape is divided into those who are 'pro' and those who are 'anti'. Using support for same-sex partnerships as a marker, people are sorted into those who are 'us' (the goodies) and those who are 'them' (the baddies).

With the battle lines drawn, a fight begins to defeat the forces that are 'against marriage'. Press releases are issued and articles written against 'those who would undermine the family'. Speeches are made and amendments and motions perhaps tabled in the House of Commons to try to 'support the family unit'. Pledges from political parties are sought that will 'uphold marriage as the ideal'. The campaigners' goals are achieved when the 'anti-family' lobby is beaten.

Having worked in Christian lobby groups, it has been a great sadness for me to see Christians operating in this way over a whole range of issues. The pattern has been repeated time after time. An 'evil' has been identified. As much evidence and ammunition as possible has been compiled in order to beat the respective opponents. In so doing, the Christians have acted on the same values as the political parties and the domination system as a whole, as opposed to the values of the kingdom of God.

Through such an approach, the truth is the casualty. Let's stop to consider for a minute what the family is about. It is not an institution to be defended from attack. There are good families and there are bad families. The family is good when it is about commitment, justice and protection of the vulnerable. It becomes bad when the commitment goes, the justice disappears and the vulnerable are no longer protected.

Seldom do Christians listen to the requests of those who are seeking recognition of same-sex partnerships. Most of them are asking for protection when the relationships break down; they are asking for justice; they are asking for commitment. Rather than working against them, Christians should be working with them to reveal the truth in the situation.

Unfortunately, the Christian response is usually too black and white. The result is collaboration with the domination system as a 'moral panic' sets in. Rather than looking to work with God's truth in a situation, we work against it.

## The enemy unmasked

Where does this leave us in determining whom we are really fighting? Jesus said, 'I will not speak with you much longer, for the prince of this world (*kosmos*) is coming. He has no hold on me, but the world must learn that I love the Father and that I do exactly what my Father has commanded me' (John 14:30–31).

Although our struggle lies with the powers, ultimately it is Satan who is the residing spirit of this domination system. It is Satan who is the ruler of the *kosmos*. It is Satan against whom we battle.

For Jesus, unlike for many people of his time, the Roman state was not the enemy. As one commentator has pointed out, 'For Jesus, the power that needed to be overthrown to usher in the kingdom was not the legions of Rome but the legions of Satan'.[4] Although Jesus' death was a political one, it was Satan, not Caesar, that Jesus had to contend with at the outset of his public ministry and repeatedly throughout its course. It was Satan who stood behind the political events leading up to the death of Jesus.

We too now have to contend with the same enemy. The good news is that, through the cross, both Satan and the power of the domination system have been broken. The new kingdom, the new system that Jesus introduced, has turned the domination system on its head. The victory has been assured.

But as we have also seen, until that great day when Jesus returns, we will not witness the final end of the system and all its effects. So we are left with a choice. Will we collude with the domination system or fight against it? Will we witness to the victory of God's kingdom or the kingdom of this world? We may be asked to fly the flag for one side or another, but the only flag that we can fly with absolute confidence is the flag of Jesus.

## NOTES

1    John Pollock, *Wilberforce* (Lion, 1977)
2    W. Wink, *Engaging the Powers: Discernment and Resistance in a World of Domination* (Fortress Press, 1992), p. 51
3    Wink, p. 51
4    C. Marshall, *Kingdom Come: The Kingdom of God in the Teaching of Jesus* (Impetus Publications, 1990), pp. 54–55

# Chapter 5

# From Wandsworth to Capernaum

I grew up and have spent most of my life in the London Borough of Wandsworth in South London. The area is probably best known for having one of the lowest council taxes in the country. By all accounts it is held up as a flagship borough. But low council tax invariably comes with a cost to someone.

Not so long ago, two of my friends living in the borough discovered that, in order to maintain the low levels of council tax, people were going to have to start paying charges for using certain local services. The charges were going to hit the elderly and disabled in particular, as they were going to have to start paying for use of local community centres.

Wandsworth council has always justified the fact that it wants to keep the council tax low on the basis that this is what the people want, so my friends decided that they were going to conduct a survey of local people to find out what their opinions really were.

The cost of preventing the proposed cuts would be a penny a day on the council tax for every local resident—equivalent to a few pounds per year. So, taking a representative sample of one thousand residents, my friends asked them whether they would be prepared to pay a penny a day to prevent the cuts. To their surprise, they received an extremely positive response. An incredible 94 per cent of residents said unequivocally that they would be quite happy to pay the extra money.

Encouraged by their findings, my friends sent the results to all the councillors, and then turned up at the council meeting on budget-setting day to see what the reaction would be. What then took place was something that they never imagined in their worst nightmares. As my friends watched from the public gallery, one by one the councillors from the ruling party on the council stood up in the chamber and began to attack what they had done. One councillor dismissed the survey as 'an A-level geography project' (despite the fact that it had been verified by an independent statistician, and that the person who had conducted the survey had recently received a first-class degree from the London School of Economics).

As the meeting went on, the attacks became more harsh and even more personal. The councillors gave out the names and addresses of the people who had conducted the survey. They ridiculed them, suggesting that this was a new political tactic that they were going to call a 'Concetta', after one of the people who had conducted the survey.

The abuse continued until one of my friends could take it no longer. Shouting out from the gallery, she made a protest at what was going on, at which point the chairman of the meeting was forced to intervene and bring an end to the tirade of abuse.

Let me relate another story that will be more familiar. Early on in Jesus' ministry, shortly after he had been tempted in the desert, he went to Capernaum. On the sabbath, Jesus entered the local synagogue and began to teach. There, we are told, the people were amazed at what he had to say. Jesus stood out from those who usually taught them the law. Unlike the scribes of the day, Jesus had an amazing authority.

Suddenly, right there in the middle of the synagogue, a man possessed by an evil spirit cried out, 'What do you want with us, Jesus of Nazareth? Have you come to destroy us? I know who you are—the holy one of God!'

'Be quiet!' responded Jesus sternly. 'Come out of him!'

The evil spirit shook the possessed man violently and left with a shriek. The people were amazed at Jesus' authority (Mark 1:21–28).

## Subversion of the system

So far, we have seen who our struggle is really with—Satan and the domination system—but we also noted how Christians have frequently been more in tune with the domination system than with God's system. We noted how the enemy too easily becomes another group that we set out to defeat, and we lose the focus of our real mission.

We might be forgiven for concluding that the kind of conflict involved in the two stories just told is something that we should avoid as Christians. After all, if we are witnessing to the values of the new kingdom, shouldn't we be about reconciliation and making peace with all people?

In one sense, yes, we are about reconciliation and peace-making, but in another sense we need to recognize that God's manifesto is thoroughly subversive: it threatens the existing powers and changes the social order. That is not to say that this is the primary goal of God's manifesto. Rather, subversion of the system is what a witness to God's manifesto—to God's truth—will frequently mean.

Throughout the biblical story there is example after example of those who felt that their positions were threatened by God's chosen people. Pharaoh feared the children of Israel; successive kings of Israel feared the prophets; Herod feared Jesus' birth to the point of ordering the execution of a generation of infants. What is going on here? Why are God's people such a political threat?

The reasons are undoubtedly varied, but from a spiritual perspective it is perhaps not surprising. People who demonstrate the authority of God will by definition come into conflict with the powers and the domination system. God's kingdom brings with it a new set of values that will resonate far more fully with truth and with God's character. People who base their authority on anything else will find their authority challenged by the new kingdom and the truth that is being presented.

One day, I was checking my voicemail when I found a message

from a man called James. He had telephoned to ask for my help. While travelling the world, he had met some people from a tribe called the Karen. They had told him of their oppression at the hands of the military regime in Burma. James had subsequently gone to Burma and supported their cause and the case for democracy. The military regime had detained him, tortured him, and then deported him from the country.

The message left on my voicemail said that he was intending to return to Burma. He knew that when he did, he would be imprisoned, but he was asking that people use his example to draw attention to the situation in Burma.

Sure enough, James Mawdsley did return to Burma and was imprisoned almost immediately by the military regime. He was given an 18-year sentence. But a large number of campaign groups were indeed able to use his example to draw attention to the situation in Burma, to the point where the military regime became so uncomfortable that they no longer wanted him in the jail and eventually deported him.

A few days after his release and return to the UK, I was able to meet James and chat to him about his experiences. It was clear both from what he said and from the reports that we had received while he was in jail that his remarkable witness to God's kingdom through his sacrificial actions had presented an amazing challenge to the military regime. While he was in jail I had also met with the Burmese ambassador to discuss James' case. It was quite clear from that meeting that the longer James stayed in the Burmese prison, the more the heat was being turned up on the vicious dictatorship. The values of love and service that James demonstrated stood in stark contrast to the violence and domination of the military regime, and, I am sure, will one day make a significant contribution to the end of that oppressive government.

James' example demonstrates how, as we stand for the values of the kingdom, we will inevitably come into conflict with the powers of the system. By witnessing to the truth of God's character, we will challenge the authority of the system. But in the same way that

James was beaten and tortured, the powers will also try to clamp down and reassert the authority whenever it is challenged.

## A tale of two towns

In the stories of Wandsworth and Capernaum, we have two more conflict situations.

In the borough of Wandsworth, a group of Christians brought the power and authority of the council into question by their truth-telling. The councillors based their authority on the claim that they represented the people, but my friends asked those people what they really thought. In so doing, they called the authority of the council to account. They spoke truth into a situation that the councillors did not want to hear, and when it became clear that the council's policy was not what the people wanted, its authority was undermined.

Theologian Ched Myers has pointed out how, in a similar way, at Capernaum the synagogue was the seat of local power—the 'heart of the provisional social order'.[1] Like the survey that my friends undertook, Jesus actions resonated with the people in a way that the teaching of the existing leaders did not. The leaders claimed to be able to interpret the scriptures authoritatively, but when someone came along who really knew what he was talking about, that authority was brought into question. Jesus possessed an authority that the scribes didn't possess. Jesus spoke truth into a situation that the scribes did not want to hear, in the same way that my friends spoke truth to the local council of Wandsworth.

The similarities between the two stories do not end there. While in modern-day Wandsworth the Christians were subjected to a stream of abuse, so in Capernaum a demon manifested itself and verbally attacked Jesus. 'Upon whose behalf is the demon pleading?' asks Ched Myers. He answers his own question: 'It can only be the group already identified in the conflict theme'—the scribal aristocracy whose social role and power Jesus was threatening.[2] The challenge to authority inevitably meets with a vicious response from the powers-that-be.

There are three elements common to both stories that we can identify, which will help us to understand the way that battles for authority often take place. With that understanding, we can start to develop a new approach to campaigning and political involvement that does not involve adopting the values of the domination system, but rather involves challenging them in a subversive new way.

## Taking the game to the enemy

In both accounts there is a proactive move to take the game to the enemy's ground. It is all very well to sit in our churches and claim the authority over Satan and the powers, but this was not Jesus' way. In going to the Capernaum synagogue, Jesus penetrated symbolic space that was acknowledged to be the domain of the scribes, one of the strongholds of the system. In the same way, in Wandsworth, the Christians were not put off by the fact that local politics is very much the domain of the local council. In conducting the survey, the Christians stepped into the realm of politics that was usually the province of only a few.

There are many other biblical precedents for this sort of action. In the story of Esther, Haman—the number two minister in the empire of Persia—sees Mordecai sitting outside the royal palace. The proximity is significant. Mordecai was excluded from power himself. He did not hold political office (and neither did my friends in Wandsworth or, indeed, Jesus). He could not enter, but he still got as close as he could.

The fact that Mordecai was so close, and right under the nose of the powerful, was enough. Mordecai undermined the authority of the system. He also refused to acknowledge Haman's own authority—failing to get up when Haman passed by and showing no fear in doing so. By his actions, or lack of them, he displayed a different authority of his own (Esther 5:9–14).

Daniel and Joseph are perhaps the most obvious examples of other biblical characters who displayed their own authority, or rather the authority of God, in contrast to the systems of their day. Joseph refused to compromise to constant pressure for sex from Potiphar's wife (Genesis 39:6–12), while Daniel declined to eat food from the king's table (Daniel 1:8).

In each of these cases, the people involved were engaged at the heart of the system. In the case of Daniel and Joseph, they were not there by choice—but whether they found themselves at the heart of the political system voluntarily or not, the point is that they were there. Their proximity itself meant that they could challenge the powers in the way that they did.

When the Movement for Christian Democracy began in 1990, it adopted the slogan 'If not us, who? If not now, when?' If we are serious about embracing the political dimension of the gospel message, then there is only one course of action that we can take. We must get stuck in. We must get involved in our local communities, in local government, in our schools, in our workplaces.

## Fear of the few

'Have you come to destroy us?' was the question that the demon asked Jesus at Capernaum. Likewise in Wandsworth, the response from the local councillors was fear—fear that the council's proposals would be exposed as unrepresentative of popular feeling.

One thing that I have learnt from my ten years of working with and among politicians is that most have one thing in common: they are afraid of losing their authority and, as a consequence, their power. It was the threat that the Hebrews might side with the enemy that drove Pharaoh to try to wipe out the Hebrew children (Exodus 1:10). It was Saul's concern that David would take his throne that led to his repeated attempts to get David killed (1 Samuel 18:8–25).

I mentioned in an earlier chapter that I was part of John Major's leadership election team in the Conservative party leadership election against John Redwood. During the campaign, John Red-wood challenged the Prime Minister to a head-to-head TV debate. I still have the letter that John Major sent in response. In it, he recalls the time when he was a Parliamentary candidate fighting a seat that he thought he couldn't win. He tried to challenge the sitting MP to a public debate, but the MP saw through his tactics and declined. In the same way, John Major said that he would not debate publicly with John Redwoood either.

It is a well-known political tactic that when you are the under-dog, you should challenge your opponent to a debate, whether on TV, radio or at a local meeting. In so doing, you put yourself on an equal footing with the person you are trying to depose. You give yourself a greater authority by appearing as an equal, and at the same time bringing your opponent from his or her powerful posi-tion down to your level.

Charles Kennedy and William Hague both tried to do this to Tony Blair at the 2001 general election. They challenged him to a head-to-head TV debate—but without success. Both Tony Blair and, in his time, John Major knew full well that in creating a level playing field, they would be doing themselves no favours. They only stood to lose authority by putting their opponents on an equal footing, and so they were afraid of head-to-head confrontation.

The standard response to any challenge to authority is fear—that is, unless your authority is based upon the biblical conception. There need be no fear of a level playing field, or even of being the underdog, if you have God's authority. Again the Bible is full of examples. On the top of Mount Carmel, Elijah issued a challenge to the strength of the prophets of Baal. A sacrifice was prepared and the prophets of Baal were told to pray to their god. Whichever god —Baal or Yahweh—responded with fire to burn up the sacrifice was the true God. Needless to say, the prophets of Baal did everything they could to invoke the power of their deity, but to no avail.

Then it was Elijah's turn, but instead of using the altar that by now was probably dry and combustible from being under the sun-light, he made things even harder. He built a new altar, put a trench full of water around it, and then had four large jars of water poured over the whole thing—three times! With one prayer, the fire came down and burned up the sacrifice, the stones, the wood and the soil, as well as all the water in the trench! (1 Kings 18:22–38).

Political processes can often seem mystifying. They can seem daunting. It is easy to feel powerless and helpless in the face of them. But as Elijah demonstrated ably, God's authority does not fear a challenge. It is no handicap being the underdog when the basis for your authority is Yahweh. Indeed, as the stories from Wandsworth and Capernaum show, it is surprising, when you work with God's truth, how powerfully that authority is displayed.

# Diminishment

So much authority did Jesus and my friends in Wandsworth display, from a position of relative powerlessness, that in both cases the opposition took the time to try to gain control over them. It is a recognition of the authority that they commanded that the tactic was to try to belittle and ridicule them.

In Wandsworth the political tactic was to make jokes about the survey that had been conducted, and so devalue the challenge. In so doing the councillors hoped that the threat would be dealt with and their authority re-established. This was Jesus' experience too. The tone that the demon adopts is initially contemptuous: 'You from Nazareth'. Nazareth was, of course, a bit of a joke in Jesus' day. 'Can anything good come out of Nazareth?' Nathanael asked in another Gospel story (John 1:46).

It is well known that the best way to regain authority in any political struggle is to discredit your opponent. Every week in the House of Commons we see this as the Prime Minister and the Leader of the Opposition make fun of each other in the schoolboy game that is Prime Minister's Question Time.

Ridicule, though, like fear, is not a problem when we have God's authority. In fact, Paul tells us that God's authority will undoubtedly appear ridiculous (1 Corinthians 1:18). Politicians have recently made great appeal to 'common sense' as the basis for their policies. Their moral authority is based on 'what everyone knows to be true'. The gospel, however, is not common sense at all; nor is it self-evident. It is a paradox, a mystery, a contradiction in many ways. Christians live by a different set of values, and these values will often seem crazy to those who do not understand them.

Looking stupid is nothing to be afraid of when it comes to God's politics. Certainly we will make mistakes; certainly we will look foolish; but that is part and parcel of what it means to be a Christian. Our job is to be faithful—and to let God take care of the rest.

# The idols of the system

Most political parties will insist that you belong to no other party but theirs. They certainly won't allow you to stand as a candidate for another party—that is an expellable offence. You must declare your allegiance and stick to it.

The situation with God's kingdom and the battle for authority is the same. As Jesus said, you cannot serve two masters (Luke 16:13). Either you take on the authority of Yahweh or you take on the authority of another god—an idol.

In the last chapter, we identified how an institution such as the family can be accorded special status as an entity to be defended from attack. There is, of course, a need to identify what is good and to nurture and steward it—that is part of what it means to be God's agent in creation—but we must beware. It is all too easy to take things too far and turn what God has given us as a gift into an idol.

Idols, at first glance, can appear wonderful. They may seem attractive, wholesome and sensible. Indeed, nothing is, in itself, idolatrous. Something becomes idolatrous only when it takes the place of God—when the values such as justice and equality which are a feature of God's character become subservient to it.

This is what has happened all too often with the idea of the family. 'The family' can be elevated to a status where the values of justice, nurture and love become subservient to it. In both Wandsworth and Capernaum, there were idols too. In Wandsworth, the idol was the low council tax—the altar before which all were called to bow. At Capernaum, it was the biblical teaching of the scribes. With James in Burma, the idol was political power and the maintenance of law and order. Each of these things became idolatrous when they were placed above what was true.

## The truth? We can't handle the truth...

How often have we witnessed our politicians beginning their answers to the probing questions of BBC's *Newsnight* or *Question Time* with words like 'The fact of the matter is…' or 'The reality is…'. That is usually a cue to stop listening or to be highly sceptical about the words that follow.

'What is truth?' Pontius Pilate famously asked at Jesus' trial. The question was prompted by Jesus who had just made the most astonishing claim: 'Everyone on the side of truth listens to me.' Indeed, according to Jesus, this was the very reason why he came into the world—'to testify to the truth' (John 18:37–38).

In the Gospels, Jesus uses the phrase 'I tell you the truth', to introduce what he has to say, over seventy times. But here Jesus makes an even bolder claim. He is the incarnation of the truth. He *is* the Truth.

Pilate's response to Jesus is a typical politician's answer. He asks, 'What is truth?' And well he might, for in Jesus' day as much as in our own, truth was twisted, distorted and often only selectively told.

Have you ever been in the position where a friend comes back excitedly from a shopping trip and asks you, 'Do you like my new outfit?' You really don't like it, but what do you say? You don't want to offend your friend or hurt her feelings. But at the same time you don't want to pretend that you like something when really you don't.

You could say, 'If you like it, then that's great.' That, of course, is the truth, but it is not the whole truth. In your heart of hearts you know that what your friend really wants to know is what you think about how the outfit looks on her.

To be truthful you could say, 'I really like the colour.' She wants to know what you think and you are telling her the only positive thing that you can think of. You haven't lied, but at the same time it's still not the whole story, is it? The whole truth is that you like the colour but you think the style is dreadful and that she would really look better dressed in an empty potato sack.

'The truth, the whole truth and nothing but the truth' is the phrase that we hear in Hollywood films featuring a court scene with a witness about to give testimony, and that is the kind of truth that we are called to tell. When it comes to God, there is no room for deception. The ends never justify the means. We are called to witness to truth wherever we find it.

## Smashing the idols

Of course, as we have already said, in all idols there is some truth. A thing that is not necessarily bad in itself becomes an idol when it is held up above the authority of God. It is when something becomes an end and goal in itself that idolatry sets in.

The question that we need to ask ourselves is, 'What comes first?' This is at the very heart of our Christian mission. Either our priority is to witness to the kingdom of God or it is to witness to the domination system. The choice that we have to make is clear. We cannot serve two masters: either we choose the lordship of Christ or we take the lordship of an idol.

The paradox for Christians who want to campaign and who want to get involved in making a difference in their communities is that, in many senses, they have to give up the desire to be successful. They may want to see a change in the voting system, the reintroduction of the married couple's allowance or an end to the commercial arms trade. However noble we think these causes are, they cannot take first priority. The priority must be to witness to the new kingdom, and God's justice.

When we do put the kingdom of God first, however, we are given a promise: 'Seek first his kingdom and his righteousness, and all these things will be given to you as well' (Matthew 6:33). When we witness to the truth of God's kingdom, idols are exposed for what they really are, and when this happens, so other things will come about accordingly. In Burma, when James Mawdsley witnessed to the truth of God's freedom, the idol of the Burmese regime was shown for what it really was. In Wandsworth, when my friends witnessed to the truth, the idol of low council tax was highlighted for all to see. At Capernaum, when Jesus preached about the new kingdom, the idol of the old kingdom being promoted by the scribes was laid bare. This is the first stage in bringing about the change that we all long for—the new order of justice and righteousness.

In many senses, God's authority, God's kingdom, goes against everything that our current political system, and also our whole social system, is based upon. We are told to set objectives and work toward achieving them. We are told to gain as much power and influence as we can in order to carry out our mission. The standard measure of success of any political initiative is how much power is gained, or how many votes are won, or what legislative change results. God's way is notably different. It rests not on achieving objectives so much as being faithful.

I have a friend who is a tireless campaigner against the commercial arms trade. There's nothing surprising about that, you may say, except that she is in her 70s. For many years she has involved herself in issues of justice, witnessing to the truth of God's kingdom. As a member of the Church of England she even stood for election to her local diocesan synod so that she could raise issues of justice there.

One of my friend's particular concerns was that the Church of England continued to hold shares in companies that exported weapons around the world for profit. She felt that this was wrong, and so with dogged commitment continued to raise the question wherever she could. One evening at her diocesan synod meeting, she discovered that the Church of England had finally decided to sell its large shareholding in the arms manufacturer British Aerospace. Ecstatic about the news, she called one of her friends, who called a national newspaper, who printed the story. The only trouble was that the Church of England had not yet made a formal announcement. As a result, £200 million was instantly wiped off the value of British Aerospace shares, as panic selling hit the market.

I did not tell that story as a model of best practice for political engagement. What it does show, however, is that by faithful witness to God's kingdom, remarkable things can happen.

God, after all, is in control. It is he who builds the kingdom—not us.

## NOTES

1    C. Myers, *Binding the Strong Man: A political reading of Mark's story of Jesus* (Orbis, 1988), p. 142

2    Myers, p. 142

# Chapter 6

# Preaching the Word:
# A New Language of Engagement

John's Gospel records that, during his time in Jerusalem, Jesus caused quite a stir at the temple, and the powers of the day were getting quite nervous. He was causing trouble. He was a threat. So the chief priests and Pharisees sent guards to arrest him.

A while later, the temple soldiers returned. They were empty-handed, and probably looking a bit sheepish. 'Why didn't you bring him in?' the Pharisees and chief priests asked. 'No one ever spoke the way this man does,' the guards replied lamely (John 7:32, 45–46).

You can imagine what the reaction of the chief priests must have been. The fact that armed men carrying the authority of the religious establishment could not bring in one unarmed Nazarene would not have gone down well. But you can also imagine what kind of power Jesus' teaching must have carried to cause such a reaction from the temple guards.

No one indeed has ever spoken the way that Jesus did. Jesus had an authority and a skill that have rarely, if ever, been rivalled. When it comes to our own mission, therefore, we would do well to consider what Jesus' example has to teach us.

There is, of course, a danger that in studying how Jesus operated, we might take his actions as an exact blueprint for what we should do. We are not all called to wear sandals, find twelve disciples and look to get crucified. The point of his actions, and the way that they are reported, was not to give us a concrete model of political engagement. Jesus existed in a culture far removed from our own and he had a unique mission. But neither are his actions to be disregarded as irrelevant.

Jesus proclaimed the kingdom in every word and deed. He taught the kingdom; he demonstrated the kingdom; in fact, he incarnated the kingdom. It is that same kingdom that we are preaching today. We therefore belittle who Jesus was, what he did, and the claims that he made if we ignore the way that he went about things— particularly when it comes to the political dimension of our faith. If we do not try to follow his example, we sell the kingdom short.

## A new language

Nowhere is this more true than in the way that Jesus communicated.

If I mention the words 'abortion clinic', what comes into your mind? For many people it will conjure up images of placard-waving protestors demonstrating against the killing of unborn children and, more often than not, waving Bible verses in support of their cause.

The image is a stereotype and an unfair one at that, but when it comes to matters political, Christians have developed quite a reputation for themselves. If we are honest, we will acknowledge that we are frequently seen as reactionary, moralistic, and not always as people who communicate in the most loving of ways.

Before the 2001 general election, I was surprised to find myself lumped together in a magazine article with a number of Christian organizations with whom I usually disagree strongly. Under the title 'Hague's Unholy Alliance', the feature in *Punch* tried to create a sinister conspiracy of right-wing Christians who were lining up behind the Conservative party. They obviously hadn't read what I had written in the preceding months about William Hague and the Conservative party, but it illustrates how Christians are so often viewed by the world beyond their doors.

Of course, it is not just in politics that we have this reputation.

A Christian bookshop near my home carries in its window a poster over which a Bible verse is printed in big black letters: 'For the wages of sin is death'.

Perhaps it is because we have ignored the political dimension of the Bible for so long that we have missed the nuggets and gems of God's story, and settled instead for the bland quoting of Bible verses, often taken out of context and irrelevant to the hearer. Whatever the reason, it is time that we developed a new language of engagement—language which is far more in keeping with and true to our mission and God's subversive manifesto.

The apostle Paul said that he preached 'Jesus Christ and him crucified' (1 Corinthians 2:2). But what does this really mean?

There is a great deal of confusion within Christian circles about what we mean by 'the Word'. Many people will take it to refer to the Bible. But 'the Word'—*logos* in the Greek—according to John's Gospel, is Jesus himself (John 1:14). 'Preaching the Word' does not mean hurling around Bible verses. It means presenting to people the person of Jesus—the character of God.

Jesus is our model for engagement with politics. Jesus is the new king, and if we are to reassert his authority we need to follow the way that he showed. This may, of course, mean using the scriptures in appropriate ways, but rather than picking out Bible verses at random and putting them on placards, we would do better to see how Jesus spoke, how Jesus acted and how Jesus dealt with the government of his day.

The Gospels are packed full of advice on the subject if we have ears to hear, but nowhere is this more evident than in the events following Jesus' arrival at Jerusalem and leading up to his crucifixion. We might call this the 'Jerusalem campaign'.

## The Jerusalem campaign

From the time that Jesus arrived in the capital city of Jerusalem, the most astonishing series of events took place. The Synoptic Gospels retell them in slightly different ways, but broadly speaking this is how the Gospel writers record what happened.

Jesus entered the city of David, not in the way that the eschatological prophet of the Hebrew scriptures was expected to emerge, but riding instead on a donkey. He was greeted as a king and accorded the welcome of a political leader. Jesus then proceeded to the temple, the centre of religious, economic and political power, and there behaved in a most unexpected way. Instead of making a speech or launching his campaign amid the splendour of the surroundings, he turned his attention on the corruption of the temple itself. Turning over the tables of the money changers, he accused the people of turning the temple into a centre for criminal activity (Matthew 21:13; Mark 11:17; Luke 19:46).

Not surprisingly, Jesus' authority was soon called into question by the chief priests and teachers of the law. They asked where he thought his authority was coming from. But Jesus did not give them a straight answer. He responded instead with a question. 'Was John's baptism from heaven or of human origin?' he asked. They were unable to answer, and so Jesus declined to respond to their questions too (Matthew 21:23–27; Mark 11:28–33; Luke 20:2–8).

Jesus then went on to tell a series of stories about families, vineyards, wedding receptions and landowners—things that would have been commonplace to those who listened. But these were no ordinary tales. Although they spoke about apparently everyday matters, they clearly questioned the authority of the Pharisees, and were directed straight at them (Matthew 21:45).

The Pharisees decided to lay a trap for Jesus (Matthew 22:15). Posing a question that was one of the hot political topics of the day, they asked him whether it was right to pay taxes to Caesar, but Jesus outwitted them with an equally hot answer.

It was then the turn of the Sadducees, who chose to test Jesus about sexual ethics. This time Jesus responded differently. He pointed out that they were in error, and then proceeded to deliver an answer that stunned them into silence.

The Pharisees tested him again. They asked him to identify the greatest commandment. This time Jesus answered, but afterwards he showed that again he had questions of his own—questions that, like those aimed at the Sadducees, left the Pharisees speechless (Matthew 22:46).

We do not have space here to study everything that happened between Jesus' entry into Jerusalem and his crucifixion, but the events outlined above provide a fascinating insight into the way that Jesus spoke and acted. These incidents are above all political as Jesus challenged the powers of his day and the powers responded accordingly. But while people may acknowledge that the events are indeed political, they rarely study how Jesus dealt with the powers involved—the powers who would eventually kill him. We shall look at this in more detail later in the chapter, but first we need to consider the way in which Jesus used symbolic actions to communicate his message.

## Symbolic syntax

When Martin Luther nailed his 95 theses on the Wittenburg church door, the meaning of his action extended far beyond the iron, wood and paper that were involved in the action. This powerful, symbolic act came to take on larger-than-life proportions in the Reformation that followed. Years later, his namesake Martin Luther King would kneel and pray in the face of police dogs and water cannons in another deeply symbolic action that would help to shake the USA. Even more recently, in Tiananmen Square, a young student stood in front of a tank, creating an image that spoke more than tens of thousands of words ever could.

The divine power of such actions lies in their confrontation with the dominant order of oppression. Within them two kingdoms come into conflict—the kingdom of God and the domination system. When Jesus arrived at Jerusalem, the fact that he entered the city of David on a donkey and not a warhorse was also deeply symbolic. Better termed the 'submissive entry', it witnessed to the values of the new kingdom. The crowds greeted him as a king, laying down their garments in a manner reminiscent of the moment when Jehu was anointed king (2 Kings 9:13), but Jesus challenged their preconceptions, his actions speaking louder than any words. His rule would be one of humility and service, not domination.

As we saw in Chapter 1, in the Hebrew scriptures the Lord sometimes instructed the prophets to use parabolic actions to convey a message. Jeremiah wore a yoke around his neck to symbolize the impending bondage under Babylonian rule (Jeremiah 27—28). Ezekiel paraded before the people, carrying the luggage of a person ready to go into exile (Ezekiel 12). Hosea even went as far as marrying a prostitute to symbolize God's relationship with unfaithful Israel (Hosea 1).

We do not usually associate Jesus with such radical prophetic action. However, both his example and his teachings about the power of symbols have been right under our noses for a very long time. We just haven't noticed it.

For example, the standard interpretation of Jesus' teaching in the Sermon on the Mount about turning the other cheek has often been one of pure sacrifice. We see it as a lesson in forgiveness and loving our enemies. It certainly is that, but there may also be a far deeper and richer interpretation. Theologian Walter Wink draws attention to the fact that the verse is very specific in its instruction: 'If someone strikes you on the right cheek, turn the other also' (Matthew 5:39). Why the right cheek? Why was Jesus so specific?

Picture yourself in first-century Palestine for a moment. Someone is about to attack you. They raise their fist and land a blow on your right cheek. Which hand have they used?

In the culture of the time—and indeed in many Eastern cultures now—the left hand was considered unclean, so the blow would have to be struck with the right hand. But a blow from the right fist by a right-handed person would ordinarily land on the left cheek, not the right. To hit the right cheek, the attacker would have to strike with the back of their right hand.

The blow that Jesus is referring to is just such a blow with the back of the hand. A blow struck in this way was an insult, with the intention not of injuring someone but of humiliating them. The backhanded slap was the usual way of admonishing inferiors, since to slap an equal carried heavy fines. 'Masters back-handed slaves; husbands, wives; parents, children; men, women; Romans, Jews,' explains Wink.[1]

Why did Jesus urge his listeners to turn the other cheek—the left cheek? The answer may be that it is a witness to the radical equality of the kingdom of God. In turning the left cheek, not only is the person is saying in effect, 'Have another go. I deny your power to humiliate.' He or she is also creating extreme difficulty for the striker. How could he hit the other cheek that has been turned to him? It is impossible to slap the left cheek with the back of his hand, but if he hits with his fist he acknowledges that the other person is his equal.

The injunction to 'turn the other cheek' can therefore be seen as a radical political statement of equality. It is also a thoroughly subversive action. It robs the oppressor of the power to humiliate.

The power of such symbolic action should not be underestimated. It can be a witness to the kingdom of God as well as a challenge to the world around us.

## Sentence destruction

At what point should we draw the line in our prophetic communication? Are there boundaries that we shouldn't cross? It is probably fair to say that we have tended to err on the side of caution, but if a prophet can go as far as marrying a prostitute as a prophetic act, perhaps there is reason to believe that the boundaries can be pushed a lot further than we usually suppose!

Recently, a Roman Catholic priest, Father Martin Newland from Canning Town in the East End of London, took part in what was termed a 'Jubilee Action' against the nuclear threat. Along with Susan van der Hijden from Amsterdam, he disarmed a truck that was used to transport nuclear warheads. But this was no wanton act of violence. Following the disarmament action, the pair gave themselves up, and subsequently stood trial for their actions, receiving a one-year prison sentence for criminal damage.

Their reason? This was a prophetic action to highlight the immorality and idolatry of nuclear weapons.

A few years ago, walking down Victoria Street in London, I met a woman demonstrating outside the Department of Trade and Industry. I stopped to ask what she was doing, and learned that she was part of the 'Warton Four'. In a carefully planned and meticulously implemented exercise, they had broken into an airbase. Using ordinary household implements, they had then disarmed a Hawk fighter jet that was about to be sent to the oppressive regime of Indonesia. Tens of thousands of people had been killed by that military regime using such weapons, and the 'Warton Four' felt that they could not stay silent while the terrible trade continued.

For both these sets of people, and many others, destruction is sometimes justifiable in order to get a message across.

As we have seen, Jesus too was apparently prepared to destroy in order to get his message across. His first major action following his submissive entry to Jerusalem was to head for the temple. There, in the Court of the Gentiles, Jesus found a situation where the priestly aristocracy were exploiting the poor. Jesus' symbolic act was to overturn the tables of the money changers and the benches of the people selling doves—something that must have broken a few table-legs at least. John's Gospel records that Jesus even made a whip to drive everyone out, scattering coins as he went (John 2:15).

This action would not have brought an end to the corrupt financial practices of the temple, any more than four people disarming a Hawk fighter jet would end the sale of arms to Indonesia. What it would have done in both cases, however, was to disrupt the commercial activities and bring the point home in no uncertain terms. Like all Jesus' words and actions, it was a witness to the new kingdom that Jesus was proclaiming.

The action that Jesus took certainly had a significant effect. The chief priests and the teachers of the law then began plotting to kill him (Mark 11:18). Jesus, like Father Martin Newland, would voluntarily bear the consequences of his prophetic action.

Does this give us a mandate to do the same? Perhaps the case would be a little thin if this was just an isolated incident. But the havoc wreaked in the temple was not the end of it. Matthew's Gospel records that after the foray at the temple, Jesus was with his disciples —the people with whom he had spent most waking moments during the last few years. You could say that they knew each other well by this point. Even so, Jesus is the kind of person who always has a few surprises up his sleeve.

Feeling hungry, Jesus came to a fig tree by the side of the road, but finding no figs on it, he cursed it. The fig tree withered. The disciples must have wondered what was going on. Jesus, who had been preaching a vision of making all things right, had in the space of 24 hours started breaking up the temple and destroying the creation.

This too was a prophetic action. The unfruitful fig tree is representative of the people of God as described by Jeremiah and other prophets (Jeremiah 8:13; 24:1–10; Hosea 9:10; Joel 1:7; Micah 7:1). Jesus' action symbolized the judgment of God on Israel, but it was also a sign of the power of God available to the disciples.

Jesus said to them:

*I tell you the truth, if you have faith and do not doubt, not only can you do what was done to the fig tree, but also you can say to this mountain, 'Go, throw yourself into the sea,' and it will be done. If you believe, you will receive whatever you ask for in prayer (Matthew 21:21–22).*

Was Jesus urging environmental degradation? Should the disciples be waging a campaign against fig trees and mountains?

This, of course, was not the point. The point was that the disciples had a mandate to undertake prophetic actions in the same way that Jesus did: in fact, they could do apparently harder things than making a fig tree wither.

Perhaps there is still more that we can learn from Jesus'

remarkable statement, however. In the same way that the fig tree has biblical symbolism, so do mountains. The story of the withering fig tree takes place between two incidents at the temple mount. In all these stories the difference between the sermon on the Mount (of Olives) and the political order of the temple mount is being highlighted. The authority of God and that of the system are being contrasted. In telling the disciples that they could throw 'this mountain' into the sea, was Jesus referring to the end of the domination of the temple order? It is the temple, after all, that this whole section of scripture is based around.

Jesus' words could be an encouragement to stand fast against the opposition of the temple authorities, which must have seemed as daunting as any mountain, and they were not just a simple injunction to pray more about it. In the context of Jesus' two other prophetic actions, Jesus is not saying, 'Do as I say but not as I do.' He is demonstrating yet another prophetic action and urging the disciples to follow his lead—in even greater measures.

That same mandate for symbolic action now falls to us. We too have the authority to witness to the kingdom even if it involves destruction of property. After all, the earth is the Lord's before it is anyone else's.

## Quiet questions

After the incident with the fig tree, Jesus returned to the temple. There the chief priests and the elders wanted to know exactly where he was coming from. More specifically, they wanted to know from where he thought he was getting the authority to wreak havoc in their temple. The prophetic action had flushed them out.

Jesus declined to answer their question. Instead he asked one of his own. In this he displayed typical rabbinic argument, posing a counter-question that put his questioners on the defensive.

Jesus asked the Pharisees whether John's baptism was from heaven or of human origin. This might seem to us a bit of a tangent, but in asking this question, Jesus put the Pharisees in a very awkward position. If they said, 'From human origin', they would lose popular support at best. If they said, 'From heaven', they would no doubt have expected Jesus to ask them why they didn't believe John. Again, they would have found themselves in trouble (Matthew 21:26).

But was Jesus simply trying to trip them up? Perhaps he was operating on another level. John's call for a one-time baptism for those who had been born as Jews was unusual. In calling Jews to be baptized, he was insisting that ancestry was not sufficient to guarantee a relationship with God[2] and challenging the idea that it was only Gentiles who needed to be cleansed. Jesus' teaser therefore calls into question the nationalism of the political leaders—and so exposes the heart of their ideology.

Jesus' quiet questions undermined the authority of the Pharisees, which was built on national pride, pride in the Torah (the Law of Moses), and pride in the temple.

## Subversive stories

After the challenge to his authority, Jesus told three stories that took the game to the Pharisees in no uncertain terms. The tales about two sons, a vineyard and a wedding banquet are stories using illustrations from everyday life, but the illustrations are extremely powerful. Here only the first two, the parables of the two sons and the tenants, will be examined in detail, but it is important to note that almost every story that Jesus told has a political edge.

One of the most effective ways of communicating truth is through story. I once attended a conference in Bratislava, in Slovakia. The conference was for Christians in Eastern Europe who were seeking to re-engage with their culture following the collapse of Communism. As the thirty or so people sat around the table and talked about the best way to do it, I was struck by the amazing stories that they had to tell.

In Western culture, the way that we often try to impart the truth about our lives is through reasoned discussion. We base our communication upon logic and carefully constructed argument. In much of the world, however, communication happens in different ways. At this conference, the main method of communication was through story. When someone wanted to communicate a truth, they related a story from their own or someone else's experience.

Stories are sometimes able to reveal the truth or absurdity of a situation in a way that reasoned argument cannot. In logical discussion, it is all too easy to miss the wood for the trees, particularly in political circles where obscure arguments can be employed to great effect in bolstering one's position.

A true short story will illustrate this well. There were once two villages. Through historical circumstance, one village found itself extremely well off, compared to its neighbouring village which was extremely poor. The rich villagers, aware of their growing wealth and wishing to ensure their continuing riches, decided that they would let only a handful of residents from the poorer settlement into their village. Even when famine struck and the poor village endured terrible hardship, the wealthy people maintained their position diligently. So the rich villagers lived happily ever after, while their poor neighbours slowly died off.

The story is true because that is exactly the way that the richest part of the world acts toward the poorer part with regard to its immigration policy. It is, of course, an oversimplification, but it brings home the injustice of our position in no uncertain terms in the context of the global village.

Given that the medium of story is so powerful, it is hardly surprising that Jesus also used it to communicate truth.

Today, stories can be used to great effect even at the highest levels. In the late 1990s, a Christian MP was speaking in a debate about asylum seekers.[3] He began to tell a story about a young Middle Eastern couple with no visible means of support. This couple, he claimed, would be penalized by the Bill currently under discussion.

The young woman was pregnant and the parentage of the child

was controversial. The penalty for alleged adultery in their country was brutal. The couple were living temporarily in a hovel, and the local despot, having already butchered his way to power, was running a ruthless, coercive population policy of eliminating children of one gender. Given the bleak situation, the fearful young couple fled with their child and made it to a safe haven in a foreign land. A home was secured, they worked, and an income was obtained. They stayed until the danger was past. In common with most refugees, they returned home as soon as it was safe to do so.

The attention of the House of Commons was no doubt transfixed by this point. It was then that the MP dropped the bombshell. 'When the boy became a man, he would one day ask this question,' said the MP: '"When I was without shelter, did you give me a roof? When I was without food, did you give me food?"'

The boy in the MP's story was, of course, Jesus Christ—someone who, so the MP said, was likely to be a victim of the government's asylum policy were he to be born today.

In his first story after the question about baptism, Jesus told his listeners about two sons. Their father asked them to go and work in his vineyard. The first son said that he wouldn't, but later changed his mind and went. The second said that he would, but changed his mind and didn't go. Jesus asked his listeners which of the two sons had done what his father requested.

This story follows neatly on from Jesus' question about baptism. John's baptism was a baptism of repentance. Some accepted it and turned from their ways; others rejected it. The chief priests and the elders replied to the story of the two sons as we probably would— that of course it was the first son who did the will of the father— but in answering, they exposed their own hypocrisy. They were the ones who had failed to repent and accept the baptism of John.

In responding like this, the political figures were being set up by the story for a monumental fall. Jesus was soon to launch the most devastating attack on the teachers of the law on this very basis— that they did not 'practise what they preached' (Matthew 23:2). Before that, however, stories had a continuing role to play.

We saw in Chapter 1 how Jesus used the parable of the good Samaritan to draw attention to the failings of the powerful. In this, Jesus was following in the tradition of the Hebrew scriptures, where stories were used to great effect to challenge the political authorities and highlight their hypocrisy and shortcomings. For example, Nathan told a story to King David about a rich man who had stolen a poor man's sheep. David was able to see the injustice of the situation, but was devastated when it was pointed out that he himself had acted in this way towards Uriah the Hittite, when he took Uriah's wife and had him killed in battle (2 Samuel 12:1–13).

After the story of the two sons, Jesus related another parable. There was a landowner who planted a vineyard and rented it to some farmers. The landowner went away but, at harvest time, sent his servants to collect the fruit. The farmers killed all the servants who were sent, and then, finally, they killed the landowner's son. Jesus concluded the story by saying that when the landowner eventually returned, he would bring the farmers to a wretched end, and give the vineyard to other tenants.

From a socio-cultural perspective, the story refers to the hostility that frequently existed between tenant farmers and absentee landlords in the first century.[4] Jesus is taking a political conflict and using it as an illustration to draw out truth. He is looking at a contemporary debate (a modern equivalent might be the foot and mouth crisis, or foxhunting) and using it to make yet another challenge to the powers.

The real point of the story, however, was that the landowner represented God, and the tenants represented God's covenant people. This fact was far from lost on the Pharisees and chief priests, who knew perfectly well that he was talking about them (Matthew 21:45).

## Adjusting agendas

The Pharisees and Herodians responded to Jesus' stories by posing him a question with two alternatives: 'Is it right to pay taxes to Caesar or not? Should we pay or shouldn't we?' (Mark 12:14–15).

In order to understand the full implications of this encounter with the Pharisees and Herodians, it is useful to know some background. There were at least two major groupings in Jesus' day that had strong views about the payment of taxes to the Romans. On the one hand there were the Zealots. Their origins lay in the resistance to Roman taxation. Co-operation with Rome in any form, including the payment of taxes, was seen by them as treachery. The second group was the Sadducees, who were very much in collaboration with the Roman authorities. Being the ruling party, perhaps not surprisingly they were in favour of the payment of taxes.

So when the question is asked, there is a specific agenda behind it. Two alternatives are laid out, and Jesus recognizes them as a trap. Whatever his answer, it appears, he is in trouble.

Jesus refused to play the game by his questioners' rules, however. Taking a coin, he asked them whose head was pictured on it. The answer was plain for all to see—it was Caesar's. 'Give to Caesar what is Caesar's and to God what is God's,' came Jesus' reply. Not only did he refuse to take the agenda he was offered, he changed the options completely, bringing into focus the really important question. Who was their Lord? Was it Caesar or God? Whose kingdom were they serving, the kingdom of God or the domination system? Jesus shifted the agenda to focus on the really important question of God's authority, which is what the kingdom is about and the central message that Jesus was bringing.

Another popular debate in Jewish circles was whether individual life ended with death or whether there was an afterlife—a resurrection. The Sadducees did not believe in the resurrection, so when they asked Jesus about marriage at the resurrection, it was a question to test him and at the same time to reinforce their particular position.

The Sadducees gave Jesus an apparently insoluble puzzle. Whose husband would a woman be at the resurrection if she had married seven times? The two options facing Jesus seemed to be either to say that he didn't believe in the resurrection, or to say that he did, but look foolish. But Jesus again disputed the premise on which the test was based. 'You do not know the scriptures or the power of God,' he said. 'When the dead rise, they will neither marry nor be given in marriage... You are badly mistaken!' (Mark 12:24–27).

In our own time and culture, we share the difficulty that Jesus faced. The people asking the questions of us—for example, the media—love to set an agenda and polarize debate. After all, that is what generally makes a good news story, and so sells papers or persuades people to listen to their reports. The more extreme the positions, the more violent the disagreements, then the more dramatic the story.

We must be careful not to accept the agenda that we are given. Unfortunately it is often Christian lobby and campaign groups that fall prey to such news reporting. Take, for example, the news that the morning-after pill is to go on sale over the counter. The usual response of a journalist will be to find a family planning group that vigorously supports the move, and get the strongest possible quote from them. The journalist then approaches the most hard-line pro-life group and print their side of the story too. This is what passes for 'balanced' or 'objective' journalism, but of course it is nothing of the sort. Rarely will you find a journalist who goes to find a perspective from children, or pharmacists, or doctors. The reason is quite simply that these groups will not give the media the extreme position that they want. Those people who want to give a balanced or reasoned response that weighs up both sides of the argument are seldom listened to, and if they are, their comments are seldom reported.

So is there a way to challenge the way that the media operate and still get our message across? The Bible suggests that there is. Jesus not only changed the agenda of the questions that he was asked but, we are told, the people listening were 'amazed' by his answers (Mark 12:17).

When I started work for the Movement for Christian Democracy (MCD), the organization, like several others, was doing work in the area of violent films and screen violence. Our concern stemmed from a commitment to peace-making and was in line with our other work on such subjects as the commercial arms trade.

We found, however, that it was a constant battle to get our message of peace and justice across without being seen as extreme. A pattern was emerging that we found very hard to address. A new film would be released, containing extreme violence, and the news media would try to create a story on the back of it. The MCD would frequently be telephoned by newspapers such as the *Daily Mail*. The paper had already determined the kind of story that it wanted, which was to be disagreement between 'pro' and 'anti' censorship campaigners. Journalists would try to elicit from us a quote of 'outrage' or 'indignation' that the film had been released. They would then go to other organizations to get an opposite quote, supporting the film's release—and they would have their story. Our message of peace-making and justice was rarely heard.

The MCD decided to try to change the terms of the debate. We switched our attention to the people who were actually classifying the films—the British Board of Film Classification (BBFC). After a bit of research, we discovered that the mechanism by which classifications were made was weighted in favour of the film distributors. When a film was produced, it was submitted for classification, but if the film distributors didn't like the classification it received, they had an automatic right of appeal. We formulated a proposal that children's organizations, and groups concerned about racial violence or violence against women, should also have a right of appeal if they thought that a film might have an adverse effect and that the classification was inappropriate.

We also did a great deal of work on the accountability of the BBFC. After some research, we discovered that the BBFC had a responsibility to be accountable to Parliament. Each year they were supposed to present an annual report. Further research revealed, however, that the BBFC had failed in its statutory duty, meaning that the latest information that Parliament had about the classifiers was over two years old.

In order to highlight the shortfall and set the agenda rather than simply responding to it, we gave the story to a national newspaper, which duly printed it. The need for accountability was exposed to public attention. From then on, when a journalist called trying to get some 'moral outrage' about the latest unsuitable film to be released, we were able to make a different point. There was a problem with the system, with the way that films were classified. It was a matter of justice that groups that might be adversely affected by a violent film should enjoy the same right to have their voice heard as did the film distributors.

# Negating negatives

Seeing that the Sadducees had been silenced by Jesus, the Pharisees got together to see if they could make political ground.

I have often heard people use the phrase 'Christian truth'. It sends a shudder down my spine every time I hear it, because there is really no such thing. There is no sacred–secular divide; things are either true or false. Those that are true resonate with God's character; those that aren't don't. The way that the Bible is put together supports this idea. The whole book of Proverbs, for example, is a collection of the wisdom literature of the time. Some parts, by their own admission, are clearly not even written by Jews: Proverbs 31 includes the sayings of King Lemuel, a king of neither Israel nor Judah.

Jesus too made no distinction between 'Christian' and 'secular' truth. He was prepared to work with the truth that he saw around him—not just the truth that had a religious ring to it. When asked to name the greatest commandment, he responded, 'Love the Lord your God with all your heart and with all your soul and with all your mind and with all your strength,' and 'Love your neighbour as you love yourself. (Matthew 12:30–31). This is what Hillel, a famous Pharisee of Jesus' time, had said.[5]

This is particularly remarkable because it shows that Jesus was prepared to work with truth, even if was found among those who might be his enemies.

I mentioned earlier the importance of listening to your political opponents, and working with the truth in their position as well as your own. This is what Jesus did. But it did not stop Jesus from exposing the hypocrisy of their situation. While the Pharisees were still assembled, Jesus took the initiative and finally launched the devastating attack that his stories had been leading up to—an offensive against the falsehood that the Pharisees were perpetuating:

*Woe to you, teachers of the law and Pharisees, you hypocrites! You give a tenth of your spices—mint, dill and cumin. But you have neglected the more important matters of the law—justice, mercy and faithfulness. You should have practised the latter, without neglecting the former (Matthew 23:23).*

Jesus was highlighting their hypocrisy. The Pharisees were not ignorant of the law—they knew what the Lord required. But Jesus also emphasized a lifestyle of active liberation. The amazing thing is that his message was still constructive while delivering an amazing critique of the authorities' abuse of power.

It is also important to note that even in one of the most scathing attacks you will ever read, Jesus did not exaggerate. He maintained an absolute commitment to what was true. This is the way that we too must follow if we are to engage politically.

## NOTES

1   W. Wink, *Engaging the Powers: Discernment and Resistance in a World of Domination* (Fortress Press, 1992), p. 176

2   J.B. Green, S. McKnight, I. Howard Marshall (eds.), *Dictionary of Jesus and the Gospels: A Compendium of Contemporary Biblical Scholarship* (IVP, 1992), p. 57

3   House of Commons *Hansard*, 11 December 1995 (pt 17), Asylum and Immigration Bill, col. 738–739

4   See E.A. Martens and H.H. Charles Matthew (eds.), commentary on Matthew, *Believer's Church Bible Commentary* (Herald Press, 1991), p. 320

5   V.W. Redekop, *A Life for a Life: the Death Penalty on Trial* (Herald Press, 1990), p. 50

# Chapter 7

# Political Pitfalls

One of the main issues that has divided Christians involved in politics in recent years has been whether there should be a 'Christian' political party.

There is an old joke that if you ask two rabbis a question, you will get three answers. The same goes for political Christians—at least as far as the question of whether there should be a Christian political party goes.

The Christians fell into three main groups when the Movement for Christian Democracy conducted a survey posing the question, 'Should there be a Christian political party?' The first group gave an unequivocal 'yes'. A significant proportion wanted to see the emergence of a Christian political party. Another group said 'yes and no'. They wanted to see the emergence of a party inspired and based upon the Christian faith, but not one that called itself 'Christian'. A third group didn't want to see any new parties emerge, but felt that Christians had an important role in working at a new type of politics that tried to bring all the parties together.

I myself have held all three positions at one time or another, but I didn't tell the story to bang a particular drum. Rather, the story illustrates one of the fundamental problems that Christians face. There are many ways to get involved politically, and not all of them are a good idea. Simply getting involved is not necessarily a good thing, if you are getting involved in the wrong way and on a false understanding of God's political agenda.

# Jesus' temptations

It has been said that 'all we learn from history teaches us that we learn nothing at all', but actually the Bible gives us some very clear warnings about what to avoid. As we saw in Chapter 2, the salvation story is littered with examples of how things have gone wrong, so it is perhaps not surprising that before Jesus embarked on his ministry to bring the good news of a new kingdom, the Holy Spirit led him into the desert where he faced three temptations.

John Howard Yoder has pointed out with great authority that all three options laid before Jesus were political. They were all ways of being a king.[1] In the harsh surroundings of the wilderness, Jesus struggled with three alternative kingdoms to the one that he would proclaim. There were three political pits into which the enemy tried to get him to fall. By looking at the nature of those temptations, we can perhaps shed light on what to avoid in our own political engagement.

## POPULISM

Luke's account of Jesus' temptations begins with the enticement to turn stones into bread. When most people read this passage, they interpret it simply as a temptation to satisfy Jesus' own hunger. The Gospel certainly records that Jesus was hungry (Luke 4:2), but there is perhaps much more to this than first meets the eye. It has also been suggested that in his literal hunger 'Jesus identified with the thousands of poor peasants whose daily existence revolved around the search for bread'.[2] The option here, heightened by Jesus' own renewed sensitivity to food, was to be a 'welfare' king. Amid oppression by the Romans, ruthless creditors pushing peasant farmers off their land, the disabled and the poor being trampled by the pious and the greedy, free food would undoubtedly have brought a groundswell of public support in Galilee. Like an MP bribing the voters in a 'rotten borough', all Jesus had to do was to be their provider and he would have had all the public backing that he needed.

The temptation must have been particularly strong because it aimed to hit Jesus where he was perhaps most vulnerable. The new kingdom was a kingdom of justice, which promised that the hungry would be satisfied. Feeding the hungry was a righteous cause. It was part of what the kingdom was about.

God's agenda, however, does not stand or fall upon whether the cause is just. The ends do not justify the means, as we have already seen. However noble the intention, it must be God's kingdom that comes first.

Perhaps more importantly, as Jesus showed in his rejection of the temptation, we do not depend upon popular support to achieve our political goals. Our power and authority come not from a democratic mandate, but from the creator of the world. A glance back through the unfolding story of God's plans highlights the idea of the remnant, a faithful minority (rather than majority) that is present throughout much of salvation history. Whether it be Nimrod, Noah or Abraham, the children of Israel or the prophets who had not bowed the knee to Baal, God seems to have a habit of working through minorities rather than majorities, 'silent', 'moral' or otherwise.

In a democratic society where authority rests (at least in theory) on the will of a majority, God's way presents some interesting challenges. The need to have popular support is ingrained in our psyche. Big is seen as best, might as right.

Christians, as much as anyone else, have gone down this road. As in the world beyond Christendom, there is hot competition between Christian organizations for supporters who will enable them to grow or, in some cases, simply to survive in the religious marketplace. You would not necessarily know it by looking in from the outside, but between Christian broadcasters, magazines, publishing houses and campaign groups, there is ongoing competition and sometimes even acrimony.

This is particularly true for campaign groups. As more and more Christian groups have formed with a political mission, so there is greater and greater competition between them for supporters who will give money and keep the organizations going. This brings even greater pressure on the groups to keep supporters happy and to adopt the positions that their supporters want them to take.

Not long ago, I had lunch with the director of one campaign group. We knew that a measure to lower the age of consent for homosexual sex was soon to come before Parliament. Over the meal, we discussed the various merits and problems with the legislation. By the end, the director had come to the conclusion that the group should probably not get involved in this particular issue.

I was surprised, therefore, a few months later, to receive a letter from the organization, announcing to its supporters that the group was going to fight the reduction in the age of consent with all its might. The next time I met with the director of the group, I asked him what had changed. He gave me an honest answer: 'Our supporters simply won't understand if we do not fight the government's plans.'

The overriding issue for this Christian lobby group was to maintain the popular support of its constituency. But such thinking should not, and indeed must not, be the paramount concern of Christians, if we are truly to represent the values of the kingdom.

We don't often think of Jesus in these terms, but of course he himself took part in an election. Perhaps it would be more accurate to describe it as a referendum. Pilate went to the people and ran a poll on whether Jesus or Barabbas should be freed. We all know the outcome: Jesus was crucified and the violent man went free. Jesus did not get the popular support—but his rejection by the people was actually God's success. Likewise, our success is not measured by the number of votes we attain, or the support we receive. Our success is in our faithful witness to the values of God's kingdom.

## I WANT TO BE ELECTED

The second temptation is probably the one that most people would readily accept has a political meaning.[3] Here, Satan offers Jesus the chance to rule all the kingdoms of the world. How easy it would have been to impose God's reign of justice and righteousness at that point. The prisoners would have been freed; the poor would have been delivered; justice would have been done for all. But this was not Jesus' way. Imposition from the top down was not in keeping with God's character. It was not God's style.

It is all too easy to fall into the way of the domination system and see our primary mission as gaining power—whether it be in business, the church or any other area of life. Even in our churches, we naturally accord higher respect to those who have succeeded in their fields, worked their way up the ladder and gained high office, but the book of James warns the people of God against taking on such values. James talks of equal respect and regard for both rich and poor in the church congregation (James 2:1–4).

The biblical way is different from the world's way. Its primary value is obedience to the authority of God. In fact, the nature of the problem that confronts us is revealed in the conditions of the offer that the devil makes to Jesus: '…if you worship me' (Luke 4:7). It is idolatry to put the quest for power before the values of the kingdom. This is why we have to be particularly careful when it comes to our involvement in electoral politics. There is no room in the kingdom for power-seeking.

It is hard to find a biblical example of someone who did God's will by trying to gain a powerful position. Many of the great biblical leaders, such as Joseph or Daniel, found themselves in positions of power quite unexpectedly. They were faithful to God and found that God gave them more responsibility. Many others, such as Moses and Gideon, showed a definite reluctance to take up powerful positions and, in fact, did their best to avoid them.

A great myth pervades our churches that if we just had a 'Christian' Prime Minister, or more 'Christian' MPs, then the UK would be a much better place. The truth is that at the 2001 general election all three main party leaders professed a Christian faith. As a result of my work, I have a list of almost 100 MPs who are either Methodist or Baptist lay preachers, confirmed Catholics, members of evangelical house churches, regular attenders at Church of England churches, or in some other way followers of the Christian faith. Many MPs are members of the Christian Socialist Movement, the Conservative Christian Fellowship or the Liberal Democrat Christian Forum. Most of these people have a very sincere faith. Compared with the statistics for the whole UK, there is, in fact, a disproportionate number of Christians represented in Parliament.

We could go on debating the quality of these people's faith. We could discuss whether they are 'really Christians' or not till we are blue in the face. The point is that getting Christians into Parliament will not necessarily make a difference. It is not our job to jockey for position or to seek power. God will give it to us, and indeed take it away, when he feels it appropriate to do so.

The fact that Jesus faced this temptation to take the power is perhaps indicative that Christians are as susceptible as anyone to the corruption that a powerful position brings. Indeed, when James addresses the corruption that comes with wealth and power, it seems that he is talking about those rich people who are in the church, not outside it. 'Is it not the rich who are exploiting you?' Are they not the ones who are dragging you into court?' he asks, referring to the rich people who seem to get special treatment in the church (James 2:6).

We are told in Luke's Gospel that a rich young man once came to Jesus. Luke calls him a 'ruler', emphasizing the close link between wealth and power. When the politician, probably a ambitious, dynamic young man, tells Jesus that he has kept the law since he was a boy, Jesus tells him to sell all that he has and give the money to the poor (Luke 8:18–22).

If the ruler was indeed exercising his powerful position in the way that the law suggested, he would already have been doing a lot to look after the poor. But Jesus tells him that he also needs to be prepared to give up his position of power, to relinquish any ambition or desire to climb to the top. He must give up the idea that if he just makes it a little bit further up the ladder, he can serve God better.

The call to follow Jesus means giving up political ambition. It doesn't mean that we can't have a political career and stand for political office, but it does mean that getting elected is not our primary goal.

## BEING LOUD AND PROUD

In the communication age where the spin doctor calls the shots, it is not fashionable to keep quiet about your successes. As the saying goes, if you've got it, why not flaunt it?

The final struggle that Jesus faced was precisely that. By taking him up to the pinnacle of the temple and suggesting that he jump off, Satan was tempting Jesus to make the messianic sign. By jumping from the roof of the temple, the centre of political and economic power, Jesus would announce his own arrival in messianic style.

But what would have happened if Jesus had taken the plunge? History suggests that a revolution is likely to have broken out, and there would have been a devastating catastrophe, such as the one that the Jews later experienced with the destruction of the temple in AD70.

Soon after I started work as a Parliamentary researcher, the MP for whom I was working had a birthday party in one of the reception rooms in the House of Commons. All his staff and close friends were invited, included one ex-employee who at the time was dating the former Page Three model Samantha Fox. Sure enough, the young man turned up with his date proudly on his arm—which certainly livened up the party.

A few days later, while at my desk, I received a call from a journalist who worked for the *Evening Standard* Diary section. (As Londoners will know, the *Standard* Diary covers the latest political and showbiz gossip.) Somehow the journalist had found out about Sam Fox's birthday visit and, in light of all the 'back to basics' fiasco of the moment, was keen to talk to me about it.

This was my first experience with a journalist, and I thought that I handled it quite well, but the next day, there was the story of the model's visit in the *Standard* Diary. Unfortunately, I didn't appear in print with the gravitas I expected. It read, '"Yes, she had a crowd of men around her all evening," said the MP's researcher excitedly.'

It is very easy to feel that we have answers to everything, but sometimes it is just best to shut up and keep quiet. The temptation is to sound off on every issue we encounter. We think we know it all. The truth, of course, is that we don't.

MPs particularly find themselves in a difficult situation. They are frequently asked to comment authoritatively on far more issues than they can ever hope to get to grasp thoroughly. It's perhaps sad that we rarely hear a politician admit to gaps in his or her knowledge. Wouldn't it be refreshing to hear a politician say, 'I don't know' or even, 'I'll go away and have a think about that one. You have asked a very good question'?

But the temptation is not just to make as much noise as possible and get yourself noticed. As Donald Kraybill has pointed out in his book *The Upside-Down Kingdom*, by making the messianic sign from the roof of the temple, Jesus would have been seeking the support of the religious powers of the time—two political parties, in fact—the Pharisees and the Sadducees, who expected a loud and impressive figure.[4]

It would be great to have the parties on your side, wouldn't it? Surely in achieving our political goals, the presence of some political heavyweights behind your campaign is a good thing? But getting into bed with the powers-that-be would have completely undermined Jesus' mission. A large part of Jesus' time was spent criticizing what the Pharisees and Sadducees were doing. It would have been extremely difficult for him to say those things while simultaneously relying on those groupings for support. It would have been much easier to keep silent and maintain their favour—perhaps even thinking that in so doing he could change their ways 'from the inside'.

Some people are perhaps called to change things from the inside, but such an approach is fraught with danger. Soon after the 1997 general election, the Conservative Christian Fellowship—a group of Christians committed to fulfilling their mission through the

Conservative party—moved into their party's central office. After about seven years of being on the periphery, due to some excellent work on their part they were welcomed into the heart of the party.

There in the central office, a unit was set up to employ several of the group's members, and a budget of £200,000 was given to them to carry on their work. This was good news indeed, and they are to be applauded for their commitment to their mission.

However, just before the 2001 general election William Hague gave a speech to the Conservative party's Spring Forum in Harrogate. I can honestly say that in the ten years that I have been active in British politics, I have never witnessed what I considered to be such an underhand and frightening speech.

Looking at it objectively, anyone who knew anything about politics would have recognized instantly that this was a calculated act on Hague's part. The promise to the British people to 'give your country back' was designed to play on the most xenophobic fears about asylum seekers, immigrants and those from beyond our shores. It may have been pitched at 'the pensioner trapped at home after dark for fear of crime' and 'the young woman afraid to walk down her own street at night', but it did nothing to alleviate their fears. It served only to focus the blame on other vulnerable minorities.

To his credit, Hague's predecessor John Major had refused to play the race card, although he was quite aware of the large numbers within his party who did. Hague showed no such resolve. From the moment that the title of the speech was chosen, the party would have known full well how it would be interpreted. Indeed, the very intention was to make political mileage out of it.

It was my feeling that such rhetoric simply should not be entertained by the Christian community, any more than we should entertain the British National Party. Accordingly I made my feelings known on the pages of a Christian newspaper. The backlash was formidable, to say the least. The next week, the letters pages of the newspaper were stuffed full of complaint from Conservative Christians, defending their party.

The story was quite different eight months later, following William Hague's departure. No longer was the party quite so keen to defend the speech, with a new leader and a new direction. Talking with one of Iain Duncan Smith's aides, who was a Christian, he was quite ready to admit what a terrible speech it had been. Until then, however, Conservative Christians were more intent on defending William Hague than objectively dealing with the issue at hand. I do not wish to place any blame on the Conservative Christian Fellowship. We are all guilty, and have been sucked into the system in our various ways. The point is that collaboration with the parties is an extremely dangerous road down which to travel.

'Don't you know that friendship with the world is hatred towards God? Anyone who chooses to be a friend of the world becomes an enemy of God.' These are the words of James (4:4). James did not mean, of course, that we shouldn't be friendly with non-believers— far from it. We are to love them as we love ourselves. Rather, he was referring to the system. We cannot collaborate with the domination system. The cost is too high and it will lead to compromise. John's Gospel records that many of the Jewish leaders believed in Jesus, but they would not confess their faith for fear of being excluded from the synagogue (John 12:42). You cannot serve two masters. At no time is this more true than when money is involved. Luke records that the Pharisees, who loved money, sneered at Jesus when he pointed this out to them (Luke 16:14). We must ensure that we *do* heed the warning.

# The two-party system

Jesus' kingdom was to be something quite different from what was expected. As we saw in Chapter 1, God's unfolding plans were interpreted in many different ways by the people of Jesus' time. A great deal can be learned not just from the way that Jesus avoided the various pitfalls, but also from the way that the two big parties of Jesus' time—the Pharisees and Sadducees—fell into them.

## THE SADDUCEES

The Sadducees were drawn primarily from the governing class and those with wealth. Living mostly in Jerusalem, they were closely involved with the operation of the temple, and dominated the Sanhedrin.

This party clearly had a great deal to lose from sudden political change, and it is not surprising that they supported both the political and religious status quo. They welcomed Roman political control as long as they could keep their privileged status and make their regular sacrifices to Yahweh. In other words, they were collaborators.

We have already looked at some of the pitfalls of collaborating with the system, and how it can hamper our prophetic role as Christians, but there is another dimension to collaboration that is just as sinister. The politicians and powers can easily use the people of God to legitimize their own political positions and ambitions. This is what the Romans were doing through the Sadducees. In return for being allowed to keep their hold on power, the Sadducees helped to make the Roman authorities appear legitimate.

In the run up to the 2001 general election, there was a new fad for politicians to 'cosy up' to churches and religious groups. After the 1997 general election, the Conservative party launched a 'Listening to Britain' campaign. As part of this, the Conservative Christian Fellowship launched a 'Listening to Britain's Churches' initiative. The goal was to hear what Christians were saying and doing, and feed their concerns into what the Conservative party was doing. The Christian Socialist Movement followed later with a similar exercise for the Labour party, which again made specific recommendations. While these exercises were extremely welcome developments, it was important to guard against the danger that the churches would be used to further the political ambitions of the party.

There is a strong biblical precedent for maintaining a healthy distance from political parties, which is found in the first book of Kings. After Solomon's death, one of his former officials, Jeroboam, came to the heir apparent, Rehoboam, and asked if he would ease the economic oppression that had grown under Solomon's reign. After consulting with his advisers, Rehoboam decided to increase the tax burden rather than reduce it. The result was a north–south divide. Ten tribes rallied to Jeroboam and a new kingdom was established in the north, leaving only Judah and Benjamin behind with Rehoboam in the south (1 Kings 12:1–21).

As the theologian Christopher Wright has pointed out, although Jeroboam had justice on his side, he still had a problem. The city of David, with Solomon's temple in it, lay in the south. So, to protect his popular support from any hankering after the splendour of Jerusalem, Jeroboam established an alternative ritual worship system for the northern kingdom. It was designed, appointed and run by himself in the interests of his own political power.[5]

The new worship involved the creation of golden calves that were to represent the presence of Yahweh, the champion of justice who had brought Israel out of Egypt. God was not sidelined; he was simply manipulated to support a political position.

It is no surprise that a succession of prophets were less than happy with this arrangement. They refused to allow the authority of God or of 'the word of the Lord' to be enlisted to legitimize human ambition. They struggled long and hard to show where Israel's rulers were going wrong.

Ironically, it was in the more unjust southern kingdom that the prophetic voice could still make itself heard, challenging the moral validity of any occupant of the throne of David. There, the distance between the human authorities and the spokesmen of God meant accountability, at least in part. But in the north, the situation got progressively worse. Two centuries later, under Jeroboam II, when Amos prophesied against the state he was told by the priest Amaziah, 'Get out, you seer! ... Don't prophesy any more at Bethel, because this is the king's sanctuary and the temple of the kingdom' (Amos 7:12–13). So closely had Yahweh become aligned with a particular political position that the political voice was preferred to the voice of God, even by priests.

It is necessary to engage with the system and join political parties, but we should also be aware that we will be used by the system to further its own interests. I have already mentioned James Mawdsley, the Burma activist who was jailed for his pro-democracy activities. While he was in prison, a colleague and I drafted a motion drawing attention to what James had done and the stand that he was taking. We then asked an MP to table the motion in Parliament, which he kindly did. A total of 123 MPs eventually supported the motion during the course of the year that James was in jail.

After James' release from prison, to his great credit he decided that he wanted to continue his political activities at the centre of the system, and so he got involved at the heart of the Conservative party. The party, needless to say, welcomed him with open arms. They used his endorsement on election material and one MP, Michael Ancram, even cited him as an example for the future of the Conservative party on the BBC's *Question Time* programme.

It was a welcome development, but a surprising one when you look at the MPs who were actually willing to support James when he was languishing in a Burmese jail for his stand on human rights. Only ten Conservative Members of Parliament signed the motion, despite the fact that my colleague and I had contacted them all. (Even out of those ten, four signed the motion because they were my personal friends.) This was compared to 80 supporters from the Labour party, and 23 from the Liberal Democrats.[6]

We should be under no illusions. The system will use us for its own political ends as and when it suits.

## THE PHARISEES

The Pharisaic party represented a more progressive wing of Judaism than the Sadducees. They were not radical revolutionaries but pursued holiness, believing that God's kingdom would come by obedience to the Torah. Developing an oral tradition on top of the written law, they applied the Jewish law to practical, everyday issues —in fact, to almost any situation a Jew might face. By encouraging average people to be pure, pious and holy, they hoped to 'mould all Israel into a holy priesthood'.[7]

Jesus, however, presented a radical challenge to what the Pharisees were doing. The Pharisees attacked him for eating with financial fraudsters, prostitutes and other 'sinners'—and, by implication, endorsing their action (Matthew 9:11; Luke 7:39; 15:2)—for failing to observe the oral tradition about ritual washing before meals (Matthew 15:2), for breaking the law about keeping the sabbath (Luke 6:2, 8–11; John 9:13–16) and for forgiving people their sins (Luke 5:20–21). In many ways, Jesus was undermining the very morality that the Pharisees were seeking to uphold.

This party comes in for the harshest treatment of all from Jesus. He is unequivocal in his condemnation not just of the Pharisees' hypocrisy but also of what they were teaching (Matthew 3:7; 16:5–12; 23:3–4, 13–39; Mark 8:15). At one point he launches such a stinging attack that it goes on for the whole of Matthew 23. In Luke's Gospel, Jesus covers fifteen verses with one of the most scathing passages in the Bible. When an expert in the law stops him and says, 'Teacher, when you say these things, you insult us also' Jesus turns on him as well as the Pharisees (Luke 11:45).

What is going on here? We can understand why Jesus felt it necessary to challenge the double standards that the Pharisees were demonstrating. But surely our job as Christians is to push for better standards and for a more moral society?

A few years ago, I was doing some postgraduate study, looking at the history of Evangelicalism. I was studying particularly the first evangelical revivals, with key figures such as John Wesley and George Whitfield. One question perplexed me, though. John Wesley was repeatedly locked out of the churches and chased by angry mobs. Why was this? If he was preaching a gospel that called people to repentance, why was he such a threat?

The answer was surprising. England in the early 18th century was in a state of crisis. Social order appeared to be breaking down. Crime was on the increase, sexual immorality was rife, and the threat of revolution and social disintegration was in the air.

Then, along came John Wesley preaching salvation by faith and not works. The threat was seen as immediate and real as Wesley went around the country telling crowds of thousands of people that their good deeds were as 'filthy rags'. His message was seen as undermining the social order. If salvation was by faith and not works, then what reason was there any more for people to act morally? The religion that was seen to be holding the fragmenting social order together was being undermined. Wesley's message was nothing short of subversive, and the religious and political establishment was having none of it.

It is all too easy to fall into the trap of believing that our mission is to push for better moral standards, as opposed to standing for justice. Much was made in the 1960s and 1970s of a perceived 'moral slide' in society. Christian political movements were born as a result, as Christians made it their objective to reverse, or at least halt, the 'moral decay'. But this is not our mission.

God's manifesto is subversive. It is just as likely to challenge the traditional morality of a society as to uphold it. Jesus made it clear that the important thing was not an empty moral code like the one that the Pharisees were promoting, but the spirit of the law (Matthew 5:17–20; 12:12). When the Pharisees asked him to name the greatest commandment, Jesus emphasized that it was love of God and love of neighbour that were of real importance. Morality cannot be imposed from the top down upon an unwilling population. To attempt to do so is to collude with the domination system.

While Jesus was forthright in his condemnation of an empty moral code, however, he was resolute in his stance on doing justice. 'Don't worry about the appearance of cleanliness, but give to the poor,' was Jesus' response to the Pharisees' criticism that he was failing to wash properly before eating (Luke 11:39–42). The theme is echoed by the New Testament writers: 'Religion that our Father accepts as pure and faultless is this: to look after orphans and widows in their distress and to keep oneself from being polluted by the world' (James 1:27).

When questioned by the Pharisees, Jesus explained that this was not the way that God's manifesto would be fulfilled; it was not the way that the kingdom would come (Luke 17:20). Our mission is not to uphold standards in society; it is not to send out the right signals about sexual morality. It is to defend the vulnerable, to stand with the marginalized and to witness to the justice of God's kingdom.

I am a big fan of the cartoon series *The Simpsons*. In one episode, Marge Simpson gets very upset about the violence that her children, Lisa and Bart, are watching on TV. The focus of her concern is a programme called 'Itchy and Scratchy', which she feels is adversely affecting their behaviour. Marge mounts an independent campaign. Slowly more and more people join her, until the campaign is so large, and the groundswell of public opinion so big, that the story-line of 'Itchy and Scratchy' is changed.

A few months pass, and it transpires that Michelangelo's nude statue of David is due to be displayed in their town of Springfield. Furious, the other women in the town who have previously campaigned about the cartoon violence come knocking on Marge's door. They ask her to mount a similar campaign, but this time against the statue. Her response is surprising, though: she says that actually she rather likes the statue. Her fellow campaigners call her a 'liberal' and go away disillusioned.

It is very easy for us to get on our moral high horses about declining standards in society. It should be remembered, however, that the very story on which our faith is based is also one of the most gruesome, violent and depraved histories that has ever been written.

Within three chapters of the start of the Bible we have a murder, and it is all downhill from there! There are descriptions of people's guts being spilled out as they commit suicide (Acts 1:18), self-mutilation and mass slaughter (1 Kings 18:28, 40), child sacrifice (2 Chronicles 33:6), a sword being pushed so far into someone's stomach that the fat closes over the hilt (Judges 3:21–22), children being dashed to the ground and pregnant women being ripped open (2 Kings 8:12).

With regard to sex, the great hero King David was not just a murderer but an adulterer. Jesus spent a great deal of time with prostitutes. One whole book of the Bible is an erotic love story. Elsewhere, there are rapes, nudity and incest. The apostle Paul even makes jokes about emasculation (Galatians 5:12) and the Bible gives guidance on how to address bestiality (Leviticus 18:23). And this is a book that we want our children to read!

When I was a child, I wasn't allowed to watch a children's television programme called *Rentaghost* because my parents didn't consider the supernatural content to be suitable. More recently, many warnings have been issued by concerned Christians about the *Harry Potter* books and films and how they might be opening up our children's minds to unhealthy occult influence.

I have no doubt that such people have the best intentions in the world, and they have a point. We must be careful to protect our children by explaining to them what is going on, and help them to make sense of the world around them. And that goes for the Bible stories as well! We should not forget that the Bible too has its fair share of 'occult' content—material that is not always shown in a negative light. It was, for example, astrologers who saw the signs of Jesus' coming in the stars (Matthew 2:1–2), King Saul used sorcery to conjure up the spirit of Samuel (1 Samuel 28:11), and the book of Revelation uses the imagery of mystical beings, magic and dragons to encourage the church (Revelation 12:3–7).

Indeed, one of the most amazing series of books written by a Christian, which has influenced generations of children for good, is based on magic and witchcraft. I am referring, of course, to C.S. Lewis' *Chronicles of Narnia*. J.R.R. Tolkien, another Christian, wrote about magic in his *Lord of the Rings* trilogy, which is now influencing another generation of children through film.

We must be wary, then, in the way that we engage politically. Our job is not to moralize, to seek power, to gain popular support, to feel that we have to offer an opinion on every issue or to compromise ourselves by getting too close to the domination system. Our job is to challenge the system, to stand for justice, to witness to truth, to protect the vulnerable and to live in the freedom that the kingdom of God brings.

## NOTES

1   J.H. Yoder, *The Politics of Jesus* (Eerdmans and The Paternoster Press, 1994), p. 25

2   D. Kraybill, *The Upside Down Kingdom* (Herald Press, 1994), p. 74

3   Yoder, p. 26

4   Kraybill, p. 61

5   Christopher J.H. Wright, *Living as the People of God: The Relevance of Old Testament Ethics* (IVP, 1983), pp. 121–122

6   The final totals were Labour 80, Lib Dems 23, Conservatives 10, Independent 1, Plaid Cymru 3, SNP 1, Ulster Unionists 5.  For the full text of the motion see Parliamentary EDM 226, 21.12.99

7   Kraybill, p. 68

# Chapter 8

# Creative Subversion

Staying in a small cottage in Wales with my family and a group of friends, we had no television before which to throw ourselves in the evening. We decided therefore to break out an old game of Monopoly that we found lying around. However, this was to be no ordinary game, for one of the players decided that he was not going to play by the usual conventions and norms. It was not that he was going to break the rules; rather, he was simply not going to play to win.

I am quite a competitive person, and my only goal in the game was to drive the other players bankrupt. But every time one of my opponents looked as if they were going under, this one friend would offer them some of his own Monopoly money, or the occasional property at a greatly discounted rate, and of course, when he himself looked as if he might go under, the opponents whom he had previously helped were more than willing to help keep his head above water.

This went on for some time, and I could feel the frustration rising within me as, one by one, my plans for urban domination were foiled. This was not fair. He was not playing the game the way that it should be played!

But what my friend was doing was, of course, quite fair. In fact, it was far more just than my own plans to drive the others into submission.

It is an odd little illustration to use, but it makes the point well. Rarely do we step outside the rules of life. Seldom do we let go of the structures that are handed down to us, the values and social norms by which we are told to conduct our lives. Most of us go through life never questioning the various social conventions. We invest in pension funds; we get married and obtain mortgages; we take our annual holiday abroad. In other words, we play the game of life the way that everyone else does.

Occasionally, of course, people have decided that they don't want to play the game—at least, not by the rules that they are given. At times such people have withdrawn into small communities, attempting to model a new way. But in so doing they have often rejected not just the rules but the whole game itself. They retreat into isolation and fail to engage with the world around them.

We are presented, therefore, with two options. Either we play the game the way that the world plays it or we don't play at all. We either work by the rules of the system or we withdraw from it. But God's political agenda sets us free from the two alternatives. The kingdom of God provides us with a new authority that means we can still play the game of life, but by a whole new set of values and rules.

Few of us will ever experience even a fraction of the amazing liberation that the kingdom of God brings, but as we recover our status as creative beings, once again becoming God's agents in creation, so we can begin to recover our ability to think the impossible, to imagine a whole new world.

I have already mentioned that I am a big fan of the television programme *The Simpsons*. At the beginning of each episode, the same series of pictures is run—Homer leaving work, Marge coming back from doing the shopping, Lisa and Bart returning from school. Finally, at the end of the introduction, they all come into the sitting-room and sit on the sofa in front of the TV.

I say that the same series of pictures is run each week, but actually that is not strictly true. There must have been hundreds of *Simpsons* cartoons made by now, but in each episode the family comes in and sits down on the sofa in a different way. You would have thought that there could only be one or two ways to sit on the sofa, but the Simpsons have shown otherwise. They might come in on unicycles or rollerskates. The sofa might fall over backwards or explode. Sometimes one member of the family will fall off; another time they will be carried off by removal men. The permutations and combinations seem endless. The creativity is astounding.

The kingdom of God is like that. We may only see one or two options for the way that we can live our lives, but God's kingdom brings a new creativity. It opens up a whole new dimension—particularly when it comes to our political involvement.


## The last night on earth

Rock band U2 have a song called 'Last night on earth'. I find this an intriguing title. What would you do if it was your last night on earth? How would it change you if you knew that Jesus was returning tomorrow to consummate his kingdom and create the new heaven and the new earth?

You might have a huge party. You might go and get all your relationships sorted out. Perhaps you would give all your money away. You would certainly find your values refocused. The freedom would be incredible, and the implications radical. Suddenly you wouldn't have to worry about the mortgage, your pension, or your children; but you also wouldn't have to worry about Third World debt, poverty in Africa, or the nuclear threat.

We are not called to build the kingdom; we are called to be witnesses to it. We are not called to be successful or change the world; we are called to be faithful and obedient. We can be these things because we know that God is in control. We know that one day Jesus will return and establish the kingdom once and for all. Our hope is in that great day when all things will once again be made right. We are told to live as if that day is just around the corner.

Of course, that doesn't mean that we shouldn't care about global injustice or nuclear weapons, our pensions and mortgages. Of course we should, but we should do so with the right motives—

not because of worry or guilt (the new kingdom sets us free from those things) but rather out of love and concern, as a response to the amazing liberty that God has given to us.

Our strategy in whatever we do must be eschatological. 'Eschatology' is simply the study of the last things, and our strategy must have an eschatological view. This is the perspective that trusts God wholeheartedly. We need have no fear of death, because we know that death is not the end. We need have no fear of failure, because we know that Jesus has won the victory.

# Letting go

In Chapter 7 we looked at the temptation to speak out at every opportunity, to make a big noise and blow your own trumpet. But there is a similar temptation that Jesus also faced later on in his ministry, which was the temptation to respond to every accusation.

Every political party has a rebuttal unit—a section dedicated to counteracting the challenges, allegations and claims made against it and its values. The news will be monitored, and when unfavourable stories emerge, they will be jumped upon and contradicted to the best of the party's ability.

There is, of course, a place for countering the arguments, particularly if they are false, so that the truth can be revealed in a situation. But even then, it is sometimes right to keep quiet, and we can afford to do this because our confidence lies in God's authority, not our own. In a system that teaches us to defend ourselves until the death, to answer every allegation, to present the best image possible, that can seem anathema. However, it is made possible by the fact that our hope is secure, and that God is in control.

It is remarkable that at the very point where Jesus faced his biggest challenge, before the most powerful person in the land—Pontius Pilate—Jesus kept silence (Matthew 27:14). What are we to make of this amazing reluctance to leap to his own defence? It was nothing unusual for Jesus. Despite the fact that he could talk his way out of almost anything, Jesus had previously withdrawn from confrontation on several occasions (Matthew 12:14–15; 14:13; 15:21).

It may come as a surprise to hear that God can win without us! The burden doesn't rest on us. Even the authority of Moses was initially rejected. 'Who made you ruler and judge over us?' asked the fighting Hebrews (Exodus 2:14). Even after God had appeared to Moses and laid out the whole vision of how he would release Israel from the Egyptians, the people did not accept it. Moses was blamed for causing even greater distress as the burden of slavery on the Israelites was increased. But when God moved by his power, and Moses acted in obedience, his authority returned (Exodus 5:19–21; 12:50–51).

# Christian subculture

There is a saying: 'Jesus came proclaiming the kingdom… and what appeared was the church.' For some people, this is a positive statement. For others it is an entirely negative one.

I never cease to be amazed at the range of organizations that now have the word 'Christian' tacked on the front. There are 'Christian' travel agents, magazines, radio stations, festivals, car rentals, solicitors… we have created our own little subculture. But how many of these organizations reflect the values and creativity of the new kingdom? Does anything really change beyond the name and the market to which the organization is selling?

In my experience, the organizations might be a little more friendly, perhaps a bit more trustworthy, but very few of them actually offer a real alternative. Christian businesses are still usually run for financial gain and market share. Christian radio stations and magazines still go for volume of listeners and readers. Their content might be more religious, but the principles on which their business plan is based differ very little from the principles of others.

As far back as the time of Samuel, God warned that this was something to guard against. Feeling threatened by the nations around them, Israel asked for a king. The reason was 'to be like other nations' (1 Samuel 8:19–20). The Israelites too simply reproduced a system based on values that were foreign to God, but with the name 'Yahweh' on the label.

This was not God's intention. Israel was to be a light, a beacon to the nations, demonstrating a new way of living. By taking a king, they took on the values of the world around them. They also stripped the richness and value from their lives. Until this point, a twelvefold 'tribal confederacy' had depended for its existence upon deep roots into the covenant and upon strong leadership at all levels of society, but by centralizing the power with a king, the Israelites lost their distinctiveness and abdicated their responsibility. The political mandate that everyone should be a steward of the creation went further away rather than coming nearer.

For a short while I presented a weekly radio show. This was around the time that a well-known millionaire businessman was involved in a campaign in Scotland concerning the repeal of Section 28, which outlawed the promotion of homosexuality by local authorities. Given his high public profile, there was a great deal of talk about the way that he had run his company. A range of allegations included the charge that he had deliberately tried to push his competitors out of business.

We decided to interview the businessman for the radio show, and put some questions to him directly. We asked him about his Christian faith and his decision to run the referendum on Section 28. The answers that he gave were what you might expect. Here was a Christian man who believed that he was upholding public morality. However, we then asked him about his business dealings. His response took us all by surprise: 'I don't think that the Bible has a clear line on competition policy,' he said.

For this millionaire, and thousands of Christians around the world, Christian mission will extend to issues of private morality, but when it comes to their everyday jobs in their workplaces, they choose not to apply the values of the new kingdom.

God draws no separation between public and private, home and workplace. Our work ethics are to be just as much in line with the values of the new kingdom as our personal ethics. The way we behave in all areas of our lives is a radical political statement. We are political beings wherever we are, and we act always as citizens of God's new kingdom.

There are some words of Jesus that are often quoted in Christian political circles: 'Therefore be as shrewd as snakes and as innocent as doves' (Matthew 10:16). This verse comes from a passage that we have already addressed in Chapter 3—when Jesus sends out the disciples to preach the message that the kingdom of heaven is near. The verse is often used to justify cunning and clever tactics by Christians who are involved in political lobbying and campaigning. It can also be used to try to justify ruthless business tactics. The argument in general terms suggests that as long as we are honest and clear in our dealings, and we do not breach personal ethical or moral guidelines, it is quite right that we should be sly and use the political or free market system to its fullest potential to achieve what we want to achieve. We live in a democratic, capitalist society and so we have as much right to operate within the constraints of that system as everyone else— provided we don't break the law.

Such an approach has been rationally and concisely put by theological consultants to Christian lobby groups.[1] The major problem with this approach, however, is that it treats all systems as neutral. It makes no judgment about whether a system is just or unjust, or indeed more fair and right than any other system. But systems are not value-free. Some systems are clearly more or less in tune with the values of God's kingdom than others.

It is odd that Jesus should use the illustration of a snake, something that so often has negative connotations. Perhaps it was because in Genesis 3:1 we read that the serpent was 'more crafty than any of the wild animals the lord God had made'. The real challenge in Jesus' injunction to be as wise as a snake is not to be sly and underhand. It is to be crafty—to be creative.

# Challenging the political system

For an example of how we might be creative within the systems around us, let us take a look at the way that the political system operates with regard to becoming a Member of Parliament. There is a standard route to doing so, which you can follow. First you join a local party, and put in the hours delivering leaflets and attending local meetings. You take on positions of responsibility on committees. You then might become a school governor at a local school, and perhaps run for a seat on the local council.

Having obtained a good local track record and demonstrated your commitment, you then try to gain the approval of your central party organization so that you can apply to stand for Parliament. Working for a short while as a parliamentary researcher can help with this, as can attending conferences at your party's headquarters so that you can meet people in key positions. Following a selection weekend and a series of interviews, you might then find yourself on an 'approved candidates' list.

This enables you to look around the country for a seat to contest. Usually you will have to fight one or two 'no-hopers' where there is very little chance of getting elected because support for rival parties is too great. Eventually, however, you may be selected to fight what is called a 'safe seat'—one where your party has a natural majority, or at least the chance of one. All other things being equal, you will find yourself elected to Parliament.

Let's stop for a minute and assess what has gone on during that process. All the way through, you have been building a series of relationships with people—relationships with the other party workers, with school governors, with constituents—but they have all been a means to an end. The relationships have developed not out of any particular care or concern for the people, but rather because they will get you where you want to go. The constituents that you end up serving have not elected you because you have a passion for the local area, but simply because you were the member of the favoured party.

Once you have been elected, it doesn't end there. Your place is assured only as long as you keep your local party happy. If you want to advance up the ranks, you have to please the other MPs and the Whips in the parliamentary party.

The system perpetuates itself. Those who enter it get sucked in easily, and soon lose the will to criticize and oppose it. Those who work their way up the system most effectively are generally those who readily take on the system's values. But it is clear that *not* playing the game by the rules, *not* being prepared to work the system in the way that everyone else does, won't usually get you very far. The challenges that the political system presents has led many Christians to disengage from the political system altogether. Feeling unable to play the game by the rules, they withdraw and leave the political processes alone. Alternatively, they play the game and take on the system's values.

As we said earlier, though, these are not the only two options. It is not a matter of choosing between withdrawal and compromise. As Christians, we can approach the system and engage with the system with a completely different set of values. Our primary goal does not need to be becoming an MP or even a local councillor; it is rather to act as God's agent and witness. Jesus, of course, lost the only election that he stood in and was an apparent political failure, but it was through this failure that his greatest success was achieved.

It is interesting to look at the phrase just before Jesus' instruction to be 'shrewd as snakes'. Jesus says, 'I am sending you out like sheep among wolves. Therefore be as shrewd as snakes and as innocent as doves.' The injunction to shrewdness is qualified by the fact that we are being sent out 'like sheep among wolves'. The system in this context is clearly extremely hostile. The subsequent verses spell out how the disciples will be hauled before councils and flogged in the synagogues (Matthew 10:17–18). The imagery is of being devoured by the system as a sheep is eaten by a wolf. Indeed, to follow Jesus' example truly, and engage with the system, we have to be prepared to undergo metaphorical crucifixion.

There are numerous examples of biblical characters who refused to play the system the way that it was set out, and were prepared to suffer the consequences. Daniel refused to eat the food prepared for the king's table. Joseph refused to be drawn in by Potiphar's wife. These were people who refused to bow to the system, and played the game by a different set of rules, but these were people who were also crafty and creative. Daniel's shrewdness in offering a test enabled him to prove that he was healthy enough not to eat the meat he was offered. Joseph's ability to offer a plan to deal with the impending famine led Pharaoh to conclude of Joseph, 'There is no one so discerning and wise' and to give him an important political position (Genesis 41:39; Daniel 1:2–16).

These people were risk takers. They lived in the freedom of the kingdom of God, but their willingness to take risks and be creative paid off. Provided we are prepared to fail, and provided we are prepared to go the way of sacrifice, the options are endless.

A few years ago, a 21-year-old man called David was shocked by what he saw in his local area. Many people had no inside sanitation; some still had gas rather than electric lights; and he could see that his local council were doing nothing to help matters.

David decided to do something about the conditions and stand for council himself to draw attention to what was going on. However, he didn't choose a major party. Instead he stood for a minority party in an area that had been held by the ruling party for fifty years.

Having no money, he went door to door with blank pieces of paper, explaining that he didn't have finances to pay for election material but that if people wrote down on the pieces of paper what they would like to see changed in their local area, he would do his best to deal with their concerns. He instructed them to take the pieces of paper with them when they went to vote, and put them in the ballot box.

Come the day of the election, despite a very irate returning officer, David Alton was elected to the council on his 'people's manifesto' in a seat that had been held by another party for fifty years. Four years later, he was elected to Parliament to represent his local constituency as the youngest Member of Parliament in the House. He now sits as an independent peer in the House of Lords, in recognition of all the work that he has done in national politics.

David Alton was not alone in refusing to go by the standard route that the party system has created. At the 2001 general election, a hospital consultant in the constituency of Wyre Forrest took on the main parties as an independent. Concerned about the closure of the Accident and Emergency Unit at his local hospital, he stood against a government minister and won with a huge majority of 18,000.

Both inside and outside the main political parties, there are individuals who have changed the rules of the game. They have not made the quest for political power their goal and they have been prepared to take risks. Willing to suffer humiliation and defeat, they have demonstrated the creativity of their creator.

## Jesus changes the terms of reference

When we challenge the system creatively, it is likely that the system will fight back.

In Chapter 5 we looked briefly at the way that Jesus dealt with the question of taxation. This was not the first trap that Jesus had been set. John's Gospel tells us that the high priests had already tried to catch Jesus but they couldn't, so Jesus was fully aware that the authorities were trying to kill him (John 7:19). Coming to Jesus, the Pharisees brought a woman caught in the act of adultery and asked whether she should be stoned as the Law of Moses said that she should (John 8:14). (The law, in Leviticus 20:10, actually said that both the man and the woman should be put to death, but despite the fact that she was 'caught in the act', the man is nowhere to be seen.)

The woman had become a political pawn in the game to trap

Jesus. But what exactly was the trap? The usual interpretation is that if Jesus declared that it was not right to stone the woman, he would find himself in open conflict with the Jewish law. This may well have been the case. We can assume that the Pharisees were fully aware of Jesus' radical teaching on forgiveness, and had made a judgment that Jesus would not want to condemn the woman. In saying as much, Jesus would have got himself into all sorts of trouble.

A trap usually has two sides, however. What if Jesus had said, 'Do what the law says. Go and stone her.' The Pharisees would have failed in their attempt. Or would they? We know from the account of Jesus' trial that the Jews were not allowed, under Roman rule, to put people to death. The Jewish authorities had to portray Jesus as a revolutionary, and accuse him of stirring up people not to pay their taxes, to give Pilate a reason for putting him to death. If Jesus had sanctioned the stoning, then he would have found himself in a different kind of conflict. He would have been encouraging people to break Roman law. The key to understanding this passage is that, like the question on taxation, this is an apparent 'no win' situation. Jesus is damned if he agrees to the stoning and damned if he doesn't.

Again, as with the question of taxation, Jesus does not accept the agenda that he is handed. Instead he says, 'If any one of you is without sin, let him be the first to throw a stone' (John 8:3–6). Jesus penetrates the motive. He exposes the hypocrisy of the Pharisees for all to see. Jesus reveals that this is nothing more than a political game, where the woman has become the victim, but his answer exposes too how the Pharisees are victims—victims of sin in the same way that the woman was.

Jesus' answer reveals the flaw in the system that makes a distinction between 'guilty' and 'innocent', 'worthy' and 'unworthy'. The Pharisees are just as guilty as anyone. But that is not all. At the same time Jesus brings the good news of the kingdom of God, an answer filled with God's grace. It is a truly creative response.

# Creative campaigning

As campaigners, we too may find ourselves put on the spot and having to provide answers to difficult questions, but we don't have to wait for a problem to rear its head before we act. We need to look for creative ways of witnessing to the values of kingdom of God. In the kingdom, we have been given a vision of the good society, the new order of peace and justice that God has promised. It is part of our witness to that kingdom to go in search of injustice and expose it for what it really is. In so doing, we put an issue on to the political agenda.

At the turn of the 20th century, a wealthy Quaker called Seebohm Rowntree conducted a survey to uncover the extent of poverty in the city of York. No one had really thought of conducting surveys in this way before, and the extent of the hardship was relatively unknown by the rich. The results, however, would have profound repercussions for decades to come.

Rowntree discovered that 'nearly 30 per cent of the population are living in poverty and are ill-housed, ill-clothed and underfed'.[2] He helped to communicate the extent of the poverty to the people of his day by using definitions of 'primary' and 'secondary' poverty, as well as developing the idea of a poverty cycle in which people could find themselves at different stages of their lives.

Rowntree's work helped the political leaders of his day and for years to come to face up to something that had previously been an unknown. He placed poverty well and truly on the political agenda in a way that had not been done before.

Sometimes, though, huge surveys are not what is required, and a simple letter will do. In 1998, the Government was pushing a bill through Parliament to introduce a new system for elections to the European Parliament. Called the 'closed list' system, it meant that, if the bill was passed, we would have to vote for lists of candidates rather than individuals.

For the many people who care what their candidates think on

important ethical issues, this was going to prove a problem. After all, several candidates on a list could have very different opinions on issues that the voter cared about, but there would be no way of distinguishing between them on a party list. The system would centralize even more power with the parties.

When I and my colleagues in the Movement for Christian Democracy heard that the proposal was being put through Parliament, we drafted a letter to the Prime Minster raising our concerns. We then sent it to as many Anglican and Catholic bishops as we could find, asking them if they would sign it. About eight agreed to do so, and we sent the letter to the Prime Minister. However, we also made it clear that this was an 'open' letter, meaning that it was to be made public. We therefore also sent it to the *Mail on Sunday*.

I didn't think much more about it until I received an excited phone call from one of my colleagues late on the following Saturday night. He had in his hand an early edition of the *Mail on Sunday*, and sprawled in big letters across the front page was the story of our letter from the bishops to Tony Blair, and the concerns that we wanted to raise.

Of course, the letter was not going to stop the closed list system from being introduced, but it did show how issues and concerns can be put on the public agenda if we are prepared to think creatively. As with Joseph and Daniel, however, it is not just about drawing attention to an issue but actively proposing solutions of justice. As such we are fulfilling our role as God's agents in creation.

I mentioned in Chapter 6 the work done by the Movement for Christian Democracy concerning violence in the media. Following our work on the accountability of the British Board of Film Classification, we drafted an amendment to a bill going through Parliament that would set up mechanisms to give the groups concerned about screen violence an automatic right of appeal. The amendment was debated several times in Parliament, and although it was defeated, the Government agreed to meet us halfway and establish a panel of children's representatives to advise on classification decisions.

God's manifesto is not just about trying to fight a rearguard action and responding to the system that has already been established. God's original creation mandate was to be proactive in stewarding the creation, and that mandate still stands. 'The earth is the Lord's and everything in it' (Psalm 24:1; 1 Corinthians 10:26), and part of preaching the good news to all of creation is to put forward positive examples and ideas about how our stewardship can be continued.

You don't have to run a pressure group or lobby group, or table a Parliamentary amendment, to set the agenda or challenge the way that things are done. We can all do it in our everyday lives in very simple ways, for example, in our workplaces. While I was a student, I worked in my summer holidays for a computer firm. In two very small ways, even as a student in a holiday job, I found that I was able to suggest new ways of doing things.

The first suggestion was very simple. In our open-plan office of about 100 people, the plastic cups from the coffee vending machine would be discarded in the bins under people's desks. There were only two or three recycling units and they were all located by the vending machines. I therefore called up the catering department and asked them to place the units more strategically around the office to encourage people to recycle their cups.

The second idea was to do with the way that bonuses were calculated for the sales force. The salesmen and women would go out every day to sell computer services. They set sales targets and were paid bonuses calculated primarily on how much revenue they brought in. The more they sold, the more they earned. However, I suggested that some form of 'customer satisfaction' rating might be added into the formula so that sales staff were rewarded for the way that they served their customers as well as what they sold. It made sense, after all, to build relationships with clients, rather than adopting a short-term policy based on quick sales.

Most people probably wouldn't consider such activities to be particularly 'Christian'. They would probably feel that they were doing more to witness to the kingdom of God by placing a Bible verse on the screensaver of their office PC. Nevertheless, this is what it means to act as God's agents in creation, to live in the new kingdom rather than the old, to work with the *evangel* that God has given us. It is also part of recognizing the political dimension of our faith.

## NOTES

1  For example, see Revd Dr Nigel Cameron, *The Logic of Christian Political Reponsibility*, CARE booklet number 2, p. 1
2  Seebohm Rowntree, *Poverty: A study in Town Life* (publisher, 1901)

# Chapter 9

# The Ekklesia Concept

For a couple of years I sat on the committee of an evangelical body which existed to promote the causes of evangelicals within the Church of England. To be honest, I had never heard of the group before I was approached by a friend, who suggested he nominate me for election to it.

Being a relative unknown, I scraped in on the subsequent vote, and began to get to grips with what this organization was about. I found the members to be extremely sincere and committed people, but I was also astonished by the group's aims and objectives.

For those who don't know, within the Church of England there are two very distinct parties, popularly termed 'evangelical' and 'liberal'. At all levels, from the Parish Church Councils to the bishops, evangelicals and liberals are manoeuvring clergy into key parishes, vying for power and influence on committees, to try to influence the Church of England for what they perceive as the good.

The organization that I had joined played an active part in this process. The meetings that I attended were often dominated by one question: 'How can we get more evangelicals into strategic positions within the Church?' The people there seemed to find nothing wrong with such an approach. After all, if you believe that evangelicals have the best understanding of God's truth, then why shouldn't they be helped into the key positions in the church? I have to confess that I found this a very difficult environment to be in. Surely the Church should be the one place where you won't find the tribal manoeuvrings that dominate our national politics? Even if we believe that one or other party has a better understanding of the gospel, is this a basis for giving power to them?

Jesus himself seemed to reject such a path, and it falls to us to follow his example. Nevertheless, the evangelical and liberal parties of the Church of England are in constant competition to take control of church government in a very similar way to the way that the Labour and Conservative parties compete for control of the country. The briefings and counter-briefings that took place sur-rounding the appointment of the new Archbishop of Canterbury are evidence enough of that. Nor is this situation confined to the established church. In every part of Christendom, be it Protestant or Catholic, recently planted or centuries old, groupings can be found vying for influence and power.

Much of this book has drawn upon illustrations from churches, para-church organizations and individual Christians. Perhaps some of the 'judgments' have appeared harsh, but my intention has not been to run God's people down. Rather, I have used these illustrations because of my conviction that the Church that needs to sort itself out before God's manifesto can be shown to the world in all its glory.

# The ekklesia

Sitting up late one night, talking with a good friend of mine, I asked him what he thought was the biggest challenge facing the people of God today. I was taken aback by the resolution in his response. He was unequivocal: 'Identity,' he said. 'We just don't know who we are.' The early Church must have faced a similar issue. Who were they? What was their status now that their Messiah had left and they had received the Holy Spirit?

The biblical idea of 'church' has been defined as 'a gathering of people assembled for a purpose'.[1] While 'the church' for most people will conjure up an image of a building with a tall spire, the New Testament concept is always first and foremost about people. In fact, when the Bible talks about church, the vision is that it exists wherever the people of God are gathered together. This means Christian groups in our workplaces, local churches, Christian charities and lobby groups. These gatherings are all 'church'.

There are 96 different images and metaphors used by the New Testament in reference to the idea of the church. Ranging from marriage and family to agriculture and construction (2 Corinthians 11:2; Ephesians 3:14–15; John 15:5; 1 Corinthians 3:6–9; Ephesians 2:20; Matthew 16:18; 1 Peter 2:4–5), there is no single definitive image that sums it all up. This might be frustrating for everyday conversation, but it is an important reminder of the subtle complexity of the truth, and the nature of the community of God's people.

Among the many biblical metaphors, however, the most widely used word in the New Testament (appearing 114 times) is the word *ekklesia*. The classical Greek word *ekklesia* carries with it the idea of a gathering or assembly. From the fifth century BC it was used to describe the calling together of all those who were full citizens of a Greek city state for an assembly in which political and judicial decisions were taken.[2]

It is deeply significant that, in looking for the right words to describe themselves, Christians chose a non-religious, political term. The word *ekklesia* carried with it the sense of Christ calling people out of the system to gather them to himself. They were 'citizens of heaven' (Philippians 3:20; Hebrews 12:23), who had been called to fulfil God's purposes. The term made a radical declaration about their relationship to God and the world.

## New church, new values

The church saw itself as a political entity, but at the same time it was to be an entity that was abundantly different from the politics both of first-century Palestine and of today. The Church was and is the 'first fruit' of the new humanity of Jesus Christ, and the 'first fruits' of the new creation. It is itself to bear the values of the new kingdom, the new heaven and the new earth, in its own life.

The *ekklesia* is the beginning of the fulfilment of God's manifesto. The statement that in Christ 'there is neither Jew nor Greek, slave nor free, male nor female' was the most amazing statement of equality (Galatians 3:28). The early Church's understanding of being a new community that lived by the values of a new heaven and a new earth led to a dramatic change in behaviour and lifestyle: 'All the believers were together and had everything in common. Selling their possessions and goods, they gave to anyone who had need' (Acts 2:44).

Baptism, the mark of entering the new community, was not a purely spiritual event, but one with radical political implications. In fact, even before the early Church came into being, baptism was a political event. It should be noted that the origins of baptism are hotly debated, but when John was baptizing people the same radical statement of equality was perhaps being made. The expectation held by many, as we have already seen, had been of a nationalistic Messiah. In its most developed form, Jewish proselyte baptism was an initiatory rite performed only once upon a Gentile convert to Judaism.[2] By calling the people of Israel to baptism too (something that was perhaps seen as a Gentile-only event) it could be said that John was declaring a radical equality between Jew and Gentile.

Baptism for the early Church was an event packed with significance. It meant taking on radical new values, a new identity and a new citizenship. It was about saying 'Jesus is Lord', not 'Caesar is Lord'. Believers were no longer citizens of the Roman system, but citizens of a new kingdom. It was a rejection of the authority of the old system and an embracing of the new. It was a rejection of violence and domination and an embracing of the way of the cross.

So great was the awareness that following Jesus meant a commitment to peace-making that there are stories of Roman soldiers going down into the baptismal waters, but leaving their sword arm above the surface so that it retained its old citizenship of Rome!

But there was an extremely serious side to it, because baptism meant putting oneself in opposition to the whole Roman system. Indeed, no one could say, 'Jesus is Lord' except by the Holy Spirit, because to do so was to open oneself up for persecution. By saying

'Jesus is Lord', early Christians were saying 'Caesar is not Lord' and bringing themselves into direct conflict with Rome.

In the Western Church today, such persecution is a long way from our minds. Some would say that this is due to the wonderful religious liberty that we now enjoy, but is it as much to do with the fact that we have lost our understanding of the political dimension of our faith? In once again embracing that dimension, would we not perhaps begin to open ourselves up to great hardship and cost?

## The light to the nations

To be a 'light to the nations' was always the intention for the political community of Israel. The phrase 'the people of God' was originally a title for Israel, emphasizing that they were chosen by God for a purpose. The New Testament takes over this title for the Christian community (Acts 15:14).

Israel was the forerunner to the *ekklesia*. However, the Israelites fell into a big error. They failed to recognize what God had laid out, early in the salvation story. God intended them to be a beacon and example to the world, not elected for the sake of privilege but to further God's purposes among the nations (Exodus 19:4–6). They were to be a 'kingdom of priests', uniquely representing God to the world and the world to God—and the Church took on this same mission.

*But you are a chosen people, a royal priesthood, a holy nation, a people belonging to God, that you may declare the praises of him who called you out of darkness into a wonderful light. Once you were not a people, but now you are the people of God (1 Peter 2:9–10).*

A 'light to the nations', 'a royal priesthood', 'a holy nation': embracing Jesus as Messiah enabled the Christian community to fulfil the purposes contained in God's manifesto, which God always intended for his people.

Embracing Jesus as a political figure means not the way of power and domination, but the way of sacrifice. The implications are too unpalatable for many Christians today. It means that the Church exists not to further its own interests, but to serve and be a witness to the world. It means that the Church must give up the desire to moralize to the nation and be prepared to take up once again the position of powerlessness that Jesus modelled. This is a challenge that the Church has repeatedly and continually failed to adopt.

# Radical inclusivity

A few years ago, European Union Directive 565 was being debated by the EU's member states. The measure sought to prohibit discrimination in employment on the grounds of racial or ethnic origin, religion or belief, disability, age or sexual orientation. Its adoption would make it illegal for Christian groups and organizations to sack someone or exclude them from a job on the basis of their faith.

Christian organizations were straight in there, kicking up a fuss. They said that the directive would force them to employ people of other faiths. They said that they should have the right to fire someone who lost their faith. In short, they lobbied hard to have the law changed so that they could have the right to discriminate when it came to the appointments that they made.

What struck me was the double standards involved. Having worked for several Christian organizations, and having had close dealings with the very ones that were lobbying so hard, I knew for a fact that everyone they employed did not have a profession of faith. Nor were their employees asked to sign a declaration of faith when they joined the organization.

Particularly in the lower-paid jobs, many Christian organizations employ non-believers either directly or indirectly—as cleaners of their offices, printers and designers of their literature or auditors of their accounts. Needless to say, it is also rare to find a faith test carried out on everyone who joins the mailing list or makes a donation. It seems that these Christian organizations—expressions of the Church—are prepared to be inclusive when it suits them, but not so inclusive when it comes to positions where the job holders might have any power.

Recent research has shown that a significant number of churches feel discriminated against when it comes to local authority funding. A common problem, however, is that many evangelical churches will refuse to hire their premises to homosexual groups. When the council point out that this is discriminatory, the church cries foul. Is this really what Jesus would have done? Or would he have welcomed such people with open arms?

This is the way that the domination system works. If it doesn't agree with someone's practices, when it is asked for help it withholds that help in the hope that the other person's behaviour might change, or to make its convictions clear. Jesus demonstrated a different way. The small community that Jesus gathered around him was one of the most inclusive that you will ever find. Made up of those who were popularly labelled 'sinners', it included tax collectors and prostitutes.

Does God give premises to a church so that they can decide who is deserving and who is undeserving to use it?

Churches will rarely accept such a message. They are afraid of relinquishing control. They feel that it is within their power to change people—but it is not. Our mission is to share the mysterious secrets of the kingdom of God. That mystery is that even though I may not agree with what you do, I will still love you and will not seek to control you.

Radical inclusivity means that we will be perceived—as Jesus was—to be endorsing the immoral, the fraudulent, the marginalized and the unclean. Nevertheless, that is our mission.

# Furthering our own interests

It is all too easy to engage politically to further our own interests, just like any other political party or pressure group. It has been a great sadness to me to realize that many of the decisions made by Christian lobby groups to take up causes or particular political issues are based on what their supporters, congregations or churches want. This is not always a problem: many of the causes are right and just. However, the primary reason for taking up a cause is often to appease a particular constituency.

Recently, a very well-known Christian organization decided to address potential government proposals to fix the date for the Easter holidays. It issued a press release saying that the value of Easter would be diminished, since Easter Day is a movable date set by the Church.

Later I attended a small meeting of Christian leaders, where a senior representative of the organization was asked why they had taken up the cause. He confessed quite openly that it was really about their constituency. The group represented a number of Christian Bible weeks and festivals that took place over Easter, which were greatly concerned about the proposals and how they might affect their bookings.

The story is similar over the issue of church schools. If you are a parent, you will no doubt be aware that in order to get your child into a church school, quite often you will have to prove that you are a churchgoer. The result is that thousands of parents up and down the country take on the pretence of Christianity in order to get their children into the best school that they can. The saddest thing of all is that when measures have been proposed in Parliament to stop churches insisting on such a 'faith test' for the parents of children who want to attend their schools, Christians have been at the forefront of opposing them. There is no hint in this that churches exist to further the interests of others, only that they exist to further their own interests.

# Tough on religion, tough on the causes of religion

The underlying problem in many of these situations is that the Church often finds itself in a position of power—for example, because it runs a school that parents want their children to attend or it owns a hall that people want to rent. This gives it an advantage that it can be quick to defend or exploit, forgetting what its primary mission should be.

One of the main places, however, where the Church finds itself with a privileged status is through 'establishment'. The establishment of the church is a hot topic currently. With Prince Charles as the heir apparent to the job of Supreme Governor of the Church of England, questions are again being asked about the relationship between church and state. The views of Christians are divided on the issue, but the Evangelical Alliance recently wrote the following:

*The fear shared by many Christians, and even by people of other faiths, is that disestablishment would mean much more than the removal of an historical anachronism. It would remove a continuing expression of the place of religion in the institutions of the state and the life of the nation. It would be a victory for the secularists who are their common enemy.*[2]

The main reason for favouring continued establishment of the church, then, is the idea that religion should be able to exert a political influence. Such arguments are frequently tied up with the idea that we were once a 'Christian' country. We desperately hold on to the remains of, if not a golden age, certainly a better age when Christians really influenced how society was run. But it is one thing to have a religious country. It is a completely different thing to have a country based on Christian values. The two are not necessarily the same.

The extent to which Britain has ever been based upon Christian values is debatable at the very least. At the culmination of the evangelical revivals of the 18th and 19th centuries, Europe was at the point of launching a huge missionary effort around the world, but when the First World War broke out, many men throughout Europe suddenly found themselves on the battlefields of France, shooting and killing each other. We have prided ourselves on our criminal justice system, but the system, as we have seen in Chapter 4, rests on values of redemptive violence and conflict, not restoration and redemption.

Jesus, for his part, was unequivocal in his approach toward religiosity. Matthew's Gospel shows Jesus urging not elaborate religiosity, such as meticulous tithing, but the 'more important matters of the law—justice, mercy and faithfulness' (Matthew 23:23, quoting Micah 6:8). Jesus emphasizes a lifestyle of active liberation—treating other people in the way that God, through his Son, has treated them.

This challenge comes in the context of the 'seven woes', one of the most amazing political attacks that Jesus made. Jesus begins by saying 'The teachers of the law and the Pharisees sit in Moses' seat' (Matthew 23:2). Moses, of course, was the law-giver. But Jesus makes the point in his tirade against the Pharisees that it is a lifestyle of justice that is important, not their religiosity.

This is quite a challenge to those Christians who campaign for prayers to be said before Parliament, or worry that the name Christmas will be replaced by 'Winterval', but who would never campaign on issues of justice. 'You strain out a gnat but swallow a camel,' is Jesus' response (Matthew 23:24). The comparison is stark: these issues are insignificant in comparison to issues of justice.

The discussion that we should be having about the establishment of the Church of England is about whether it is just or fair. Justice, not religion, was to be the hallmark of the new *ekklesia*. Is it fair that, by virtue of establishment, 26 unelected bishops sit in the House of Lords? In a democratic society, there is a strong case for arguing that this is not a just situation at all.

# Leading by example

In all these things, living as the new *ekklesia* of God means recognizing that the Church has a responsibility to lead by example. Its every action is a political statement that speaks about the new kingdom.

In recent years, there has been a great deal of debate about 'standards' in national life. Following the 'cash for questions' affair, there have repeated allegations about the donations made to individual MPs and to parties in return for political influence. It should not really surprise us: it has been going on for years. It's the way that the system works, after all.

The result has been a substantial shake-up of the way that things are done. However, at the time when the new rules were coming in—rules that would require political parties to declare the donors of sums over £5,000—the internet web portal *Xalt.co.uk* decided that it would be interesting to find out the views of Christian political and campaigning groups on the subject.

*Xalt* surveyed twenty of the biggest Christian campaigning and lobby groups, asking them three questions. The first question was whether they would be prepared to make public the names of the donors who had given over £5,000 towards their work. It was somewhat surprising to find that only ten per cent would be prepared to reveal this information.

The organizations were then asked for their reasons. The majority cited the need to protect their donors' privacy, or saw no reason to declare the sources of major funding. A large proportion of the groups contacted felt that it was right to protect the anonymity of their donors, despite the fact that their work involved campaigning and lobbying for legislative change. Many of the groups also sounded uneasy when questioned on the subject—with some being unwilling to discuss the matter at all. Regardless of whether we feel that it is right for Christian groups involved in political activities to declare the sources of major funding, the uneasiness about such questions demonstrates that a debate among Christians now needs to take place.

The groups were also asked whether they would be prepared to consider changing their policies in light of recent events. Several declined to comment and none were prepared to change their policies.

If Christians are to call for the highest standards from those in public life, we should certainly be examining and discussing our own standards and attitudes. If the people of God are indeed to be the *ekklesia* that God intended, we will need to follow through the intentions that God has for the Church, and lead by example. This means demonstrating in our own activities a desire at least to do things differently.

# Conclusion

Thankfully, it does seem that many Christians are making a sincere effort to communicate their activities to the outside world. Over the last few years there has been a trend, not just in the Church but in government too, to recognize the contribution being made by churches to the well-being of society.

Church schools, it is argued, are good because they get the best results. Stable family relationships should be supported because they provide the best environment for children. These are all legitimate arguments to push in the public square, but they must not be pushed too far. Ultimately we believe that these things are valid not because they work, but because they are in harmony with the character of God. This is where their authority comes from.

We may claim that our faith works—that as Christians we can do the business—but the fact is that our *evangel*, the good news of the gospel, does not always do so in the way that policy-makers or politicians expect or would want. Our faith is a faith of justice, of peace-making and of equality, but it is also a faith of confrontation, of challenge and of change. God has a subversive manifesto that challenges the old order and brings in a new one. It is not something that will automatically endear us to the surrounding world, but that, nevertheless, is God's political agenda.

## NOTES

1    Workshop notes, *02 Community and Faith–04 The Church* (Anvil Trust), p. 2
2    Workshop notes, *The Church* (Anvil Trust), p. 5
3    *Dictionary of Jesus and the Gospels*, p. 56
4    *PQ Christian Perspectives on Public Affairs*, Vol 1 number 10, 13 June 2001 (Evangelical Alliance)

Also from BRF

# Urban God

## Bible readings and comment on living in the city
## John Proctor

*Urban God* combs the Bible for stories about cities, and finds many echoes between Bible times and city living today. The Bible speaks well of urban life, and of how good it can be with God. There is plenty of realism, too, about what a mess a city can be without God. In cities, like everywhere else, human life is mixed material: made by God, marred by our mistakes, and yet constantly beckoned to the promise of God's renewing love. God believes in cities—but it also matters that cities believe in God.

So read God's story in the Bible, and hold it alongside your own. Let scripture teach you more of what God sees, enjoys and longs for in your place. And read the Bible with sharper eyes, because the God you meet in its pages is the God you serve in the days and duties of your own life.

*ISBN 1 84101 256 4   £5.99*

To order a copy of this book, see the order form on page 159.

# The Challenge of Cell Church

## Getting to grips with cell church values
## Phil Potter

*The Challenge of Cell Church* is the book for all those who are puzzled but intrigued by the mention of cell church. Author Phil Potter explains how tapping into the hidden potential of small groups can help your church grow. Sharing his own experience, he covers issues including shared ministry, discipling, communication, community, evangelism, prayer and worship.

*The Challenge of Cell Church* is packed with practical insight for leaders who want to get involved in cell church. Each chapter includes a cell study outline for home groups and leadership teams, helping them to reflect on the life and health of their own small groups. A helpful appendix offers a range of practical ideas for growing cells.

*ISBN 1 84101 218 1   £6.99*

To order a copy of this book, see the order form on page 159.

# Dream Stories

## A journey into the Bible's dreams and visions
## Russ Parker

Dreams have fascinated humanity for thousands of years. In today's sceptical culture, we tend to dismiss dreams as having little or no importance, yet almost everybody has at least one dream they remember which may have had an effect upon them, sometimes lasting for many years.

In the Bible, dreams and visions were seen as powerful ways in which God communicated with his people. Prophets, early leaders of the Christian Church, and rulers of foreign powers experienced dreams that had impact and consequence for the dreamer and those about him.

*Dream Stories* takes a look at how God spoke to his people through their dreams, from Jacob's dream at Bethel to Paul's night-time vision calling him to Macedonia. Russ Parker draws on twenty years' experience of pastoral ministry and examines these stories, showing how God still speaks to us through our dreams, bringing fresh opportunities for healing and growth.

*ISBN 1 84101 072 3   £6.99*

To order a copy of this book, see the order form on page 159.

*Guidelines* is a unique Bible reading resource that offers four months of in-depth study written by leading scholars. Contributors are drawn from around the world, as well as the UK, and represent a stimulating and thought-provoking breadth of Christian tradition.

Instead of the usual dated daily readings, *Guidelines* provides weekly units, broken into at least six sections, plus an introduction giving context for the passage, and a final section of points for thought and prayer. On any day you can read as many or as few sections as you wish, to fit in with work or home routine. As well as a copy of *Guidelines*, you will need a Bible. Each contributor also suggests books for further study.

## GUIDELINES SUBSCRIPTIONS

❏ I would like to give a gift subscription
  (please complete both name and address sections below)
❏ I would like to take out a subscription myself
  (complete name and address details only once)

This completed coupon should be sent with appropriate payment to BRF. Alternatively, please write to us quoting your name, address, the subscription you would like for either yourself or a friend (with their name and address), the start date and credit card number, expiry date and signature if paying by credit card.

Gift subscription name _____

Gift subscription address _____

_____ Postcode _____

**Please send to the above, beginning with the next January/May/September\* issue.**
**(\* *delete as applicable*)**

| (please tick box) | UK | SURFACE | AIR MAIL |
|---|---|---|---|
| GUIDELINES | ❏ £11.10 | ❏ £12.45 | ❏ £14.70 |
| GUIDELINES 3-year sub | ❏ £27.45 | | |

Please complete the payment details below and send your coupon, with appropriate payment to: **BRF, First Floor, Elsfield Hall, 15–17 Elsfield Way, Oxford OX2 8FG**

Your name _____

Your address _____

_____ Postcode _____

Total enclosed £ _____ (cheques should be made payable to 'BRF')

Payment by cheque ❏ postal order ❏ Visa ❏ Mastercard ❏ Switch ❏

Card number: ☐☐☐☐ ☐☐☐☐ ☐☐☐☐ ☐☐☐☐

Expiry date of card: ☐☐☐☐   Issue number (Switch): ☐☐☐☐

Signature (essential if paying by credit/Switch card) _____

NB: BRF notes are also available from your local Christian bookshop.   **BRF is a Registered Charity**

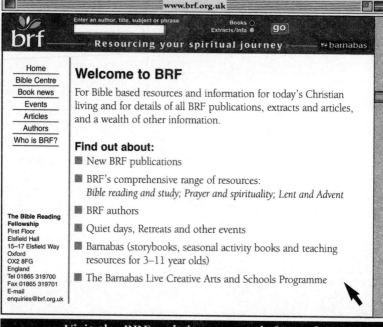